My Teacher Glows in the Dark
.
My Teacher Flunked the Planet

MY TEACHER
Glows in the Dark

MY TEACHER
Flunked the Planet

Ann Hodgman

My Teacher Glows in the Dark
was first published in the USA by Simon & Schuster Inc.
first published in the UK in Lions in 1991.
My Teacher Flunked the Planet
was first published in the USA by Simon & Schuster Inc.
First published in the UK in Lions in 1992.
This edition specially produced for School Book Fairs in 1994

2 4 6 8 10 9 7 5 3 1

Lions is an imprint of the Children's Division,
part of HarperCollins Publishers Ltd,
77/85 Fulham Palace Road,
Hammersmith, London W6 8JB.

© General Licensing Company, Inc. 1991 and 1992

The author asserts the moral right to be
identified as the author of this work

ISBN 0 00 679141 7

Printed and bound in Great Britain by
HarperCollins Manufacturing, Glasgow

MY TEACHER
Glows IN THE Dark

For Trisha Hamilton,
who cared

CHAPTER ONE

I Choose the Stars

So there we were—Susan Simmons, Duncan Dougal, and me, Peter Thompson—sitting in an alien spaceship the size of New Jersey, waiting to learn how we were supposed to save the world, when Susan said, "All right, Peter, give."

"Beg your pardon?" I asked innocently.

"Tell us what's been going on! Five months ago you took off for outer space with Broxholm. Five minutes ago you showed up in a beam of blue light and told Duncan and me we had to help you save the world. I want to know what happened in between."

"Me, too!" said Duncan.

Five months ago I wouldn't have cared what Duncan Dougal thought. As far as I was concerned, he was the world's biggest snotball, a kid whose main hobbies were drooling on his homework, farting in class, and beating me up. I thought he was as likable as a mosquito, as friendly as a rattlesnake, and as useful as a screen door in a spaceship.

But that was before I got a good look at the

inside of his head—which was less frightening and more sad than I ever would have guessed.

"Well, since you asked . . ." I drawled.

"Peter," snapped Susan, "for five months every kid in Kennituck Falls has been dying to know what happened to you after you went off with Broxholm. Stop stalling and tell the story, or you're going to be very sorry!"

So I told them. But that wasn't good enough. Oh, no. Now they insist I have to write it down. "We wrote about our part," they keep saying. "Now it's *your* turn."

So here goes:

As you probably know, it all started when this alien named Broxholm wanted to kidnap five kids from our sixth grade class last spring. He started by trapping our real teacher, Ms. Schwartz, in a force field. He kept her in his attic while he disguised himself as a substitute teacher named Mr. Smith and took over our class.

One day Susan followed Mr. Smith home and saw him peel off his face. Underneath his human mask was a green-skinned, orange-eyed alien.

Susan came to me for help, mostly because she didn't think anyone else would believe her. She thought *I* might because I used to read so much science fiction.

The two of us spent days trying to figure out how to stop Broxholm. One night I was sitting home alone, eating a can of cold beans and wondering where my father was, when it hit me that if we *couldn't* stop Broxholm, if some kids *had* to go into space, I might as well be one of them. It wouldn't be any worse than staying where I was. And it might be better.

I was frightened by the idea, of course. But I didn't think the aliens were going to dissect my brain or anything like that. In fact, I figured *I* might learn as much from them as they did from me.

That was the key, I guess; I knew I could learn something. That was important to me, since learning is the one thing I really like. If that sounds strange, look at it like this: if other kids treated *you* like a nerd and a geek all the time, if you went for weeks feeling like books were *your* only friends—well, you might really be into learning, too.

Anyway, between being the school dumping ground for emotional toxic waste and having a father who didn't give two bags of llama droppings whether I was alive or dead, I figured I didn't have much to lose by going with Broxholm.

Besides, more than anything else in the world, I wanted to travel to the stars and explore other planets.

That's why when Susan and the school band overpowered the alien on the night of our spring concert, I slipped around back to help him escape.

After I let Broxholm out, he turned and used something that looked like a pencil to *melt* the door shut.

Oh, oh, I thought. *Now you're in for it, Peter.*

But then I thought, *Well, wait a minute. If he has a weapon like that, he could have fried the whole crowd.*

Since he *hadn't,* I figured he wasn't going to make me into sausage; at least, not right away.

So when he started to run, I began to run alongside him.

"What are you doing?" cried the alien.

"I want to come with you!"

I think Broxholm would have stopped running right then, if he had figured it was safe. It wasn't, so he kept going. He was in good shape; I didn't hear him pant or gasp for breath at all. (Of course, for all I knew, when people from his planet got tired it made their armpits ache.)

Three blocks from the school he stopped running.

Then he disappeared.

I felt like my heart had disappeared, too. Never mind that Broxholm was a lean, green kidnapper from outer space. He was going back to the stars, and I wanted to go with him.

"Broxholm!" I yelled. "Wait! Take me!"

4

"Be quiet while I adjust this!" snapped a voice beside me.

An instant later I disappeared, too. Which is to say, I became invisible because of something Broxholm did.

"Wow," I whispered, looking down at where I used to be, "that's *awesome!*"

"Shut up, or you stay here," growled Broxholm.

I shut up. I may have saved his bacon back at the school, and I may have been the only one willing to go with him, but I figured if I got in the way of his escape, Broxholm would dump me faster than my mother had dumped my father when something better came along.

"Now, follow me," whispered Broxholm.

"How? I can't see you!"

After a moment of silence, I felt strong hands grab me by the waist. "Stay quiet!" hissed Broxholm as he tossed me over his shoulder. It reminded me of the first day I had met him, when he picked up Duncan and me to stop us from fighting.

He started to run. He was amazingly fast.

When we reached the little house where Broxholm had been living, he made us both visible again. Turning to me, he said, "I have some things to do before we can go. I also owe you a favor. Here it is: you have three minutes to change your mind. Otherwise, you're coming with me."

Before I could say a thing, he walked away—leaving me alone to make the biggest decision of my life.

Back at school that decision had been easy. Lying in my bed, in my empty house, I had known for sure what I would do. But this wasn't just some wishing game anymore. It was real.

I thought about my father. Would he miss me? Probably. At least, for a little while. Then he'd probably be just as glad I was gone; one less nuisance for him to cope with.

I thought about school, where I spent most of my time trying not to get beat up by Duncan and other jerks who thought being smart was a crime.

My life would have been a lot different if it was okay to be smart in school. But it's not. It's okay to be pretty smart. But not *real* smart—which is kind of stupid when you think about it. I mean, all these guys picking on smart kids and calling them geeks and dweebs are going to grow up and want to know why *they* don't *do something* about the terrible state the world is in.

I can tell you why. By the time they grow up, most of the kids who really could have changed things are wrecked.

I'll bet you this very minute, even while you're reading these words, some kid who's bright enough to cure cancer when he or she grows up is getting hassled for being an "egghead."

Any takers?

Anyway, I had plenty of reasons to run away. But that wasn't what made up my mind. I didn't just want to run away; I wanted to run *to* something. And that something was space.

I thought about my father again, and wondered if he had ever loved me.

I thought about the stars, and the secrets they held.

Broxholm walked into the kitchen, carrying a large wooden box and two flat pieces of plastic. I recognized the pieces of plastic: they were part of his communication system. Later I found out that the box was his dressing table, all folded up.

"Well?" he asked.

My hands were trembling like a pair of gerbils that had just been dropped into a snake pit. Some of that was terror; some of it was pure excitement. Looking straight into his huge orange eyes, I whispered, "I'm coming with you."

CHAPTER TWO

The Cellar Beneath the Cellar

Broxholm didn't congratulate me, or thank me, or say he was glad to have me along. He just nodded, said, "Follow me," and started toward the cellar door.

The cellar was pretty much as I remembered it from the times I had snuck in with Susan. But Broxholm surprised me. When we reached the far wall, he pressed his hand against a concrete block. A section of the floor tilted back. Blue-gray light streamed up through the opening.

"You first," he said, nodding toward the hole.

Swallowing hard, I approached the light. Then I looked down, and my fear was washed away in wonder. The trapdoor led to an enormous chamber; in the chamber was a spaceship.

A stairway curved along the side of the chamber. I scrambled down the steps. Broxholm was close behind me.

This second cellar was as polished as the first had been rough. The soft light that filled it came from the wall itself. I say wall because that's all the room had—a single gently curving wall with no edges and no corners. When I put my hand against it, it felt smooth, and slightly warm.

I felt like I was inside an egg.

Still, it was the ship that took most of my attention. Staring at it, I felt such a wave of joy that I thought I might float right off the floor. This was more than my ticket off a planet where I'd never been very happy; it was the key to the stars, and everything I'd dreamed of.

The top of the ship was a half sphere. This rested on a base that looked like a fifty-foot-wide soup bowl surrounded by a ring of lights. The base tapered down in layers, a little like a kid's toy top.

Broxholm whistled three harsh notes and an opening appeared in the side of the ship. A long strip of silvery metal stretched down to where we stood. Turning to me, Broxholm said: "Enter."

I stepped onto the silvery plank. It started to move. Feeling as if the ship was about to swallow me, I jumped back.

"Hurry!" snapped Broxholm.

I ran up the plank.

Once inside, I was aching to look around. But Broxholm hustled me to a platform that floated us up to the next level.

"Sit," he said, pointing toward one of four large chairs.

I sat. The padding on the chair was comfortable.

Taking a seat near me, Broxholm pushed a couple of buttons. Part of the curved wall slid aside. He laid his hand on a glowing pad. The ship began to slide forward, into a dark area. Suddenly we started to float. I was afraid we were going to hit the ceiling. But at the last possible moment, Broxholm's *entire back yard* flipped up, like a giant trap door.

As we lifted away I saw cop cars racing toward the house. One stopped. The door flew open and a blond kid scrambled out.

"Susan!" I cried.

She couldn't hear me, of course. That didn't

stop me from making a fool of myself. Seeing her
made me remember that not *everything* down
there was rotten. "Wait!" I cried, turning to Broxholm. "Wait. I want to go back!"

Broxholm didn't even look at me as he moved
his hands over the control panel. "There's no
turning back now," he snapped.

The ship began to move faster. I watched the
earth drop away beneath us. Within seconds I had
lost sight of Susan, the house, even the town.

I felt hollow inside.

"Stop that," said Broxholm. He shook his head.
"You earthlings! You never know what you
want. If you'd stop trying to hold on to *everything*, you'd be a lot happier."

11

It wasn't until he spoke that I realized I was crying. "Sorry," I whispered, wiping my eyes with the back of my hand.

Broxholm touched my shoulder. "Don't look back," he said softly. "Look up!"

When I did, I started to cry again—this time out of sheer joy. We were heading for the moon. Beyond it lay the void of outer space, a deep black sprinkled with stars.

The moon continued to grow in the viewing space.

"We're going awfully fast, aren't we?" I asked after a moment.

"Compared to what?"

"Well, compared to earth rockets."

"Yes."

The guy was not much of a conversationalist. I was about to ask why the acceleration hadn't pushed me into my seat when we began to make a curve around the moon. When we got to the other side, I was astonished into silence myself.

One problem with writing about aliens is that sometimes it gets hard to describe things. For example, if I say that what I saw now was the biggest thing I had ever seen in my life, that wouldn't be true. A lot of things in nature—like the sun, the moon, and the stars—are bigger.

But if I say it was the biggest man-made thing I ever saw, that wouldn't be true either, because this wasn't made by men—or women, for that matter. It was made by aliens. And it was enormous—a huge lavender sphere that made Broxholm's ship look like an ant on the face of Mount Rushmore.

"What is that?" I finally managed to whisper.

"The good ship *New Jersey*," replied Broxholm.

I blinked. "The *New Jersey*?"

Broxholm pulled on his nose, which stretched out to about twice its normal length, then snapped back into place. I learned later that this is what people on his planet do instead of sighing.

"One of the senior members of our ship's crew has a rather bizarre sense of humor," said Broxholm. "This crew member has also spent a lot of time studying your planet. When the ship was built, it decided that since the ship's surface area was equal to that of New Jersey, that should be the name of the ship. Not everyone was amused."

"The ship decided?" I asked in puzzlement.

"No, the crew member," said Broxholm.

"But you said 'it' decided."

"That's because I'm wearing an implant that translates everything I say into English, and no pronoun in your language properly describes this crew member, who is neither a he nor a she, but something else all together."

"What else is there?"

Broxholm pulled on his nose again. "This crewperson comes from a planet where it takes five different genders just to get an egg—and three more to hatch it."

My mind was starting to spin. But before I could ask more questions, a hole opened in the side of the great sphere and a multicolored beam of light extended to our little vessel.

"Docking beam," said Broxholm, pointing to the light. "Soon we'll be inside. Then the fun begins."

"Fun?"

"Sarcasm," said Broxholm softly. "I will have to explain why you are with me. That will not be fun. Not at all."

CHAPTER THREE

The Naked Stranger

Sarcasm? Did that mean Broxholm had a sense of humor? The idea fascinated me. But this didn't seem like the time to ask about it, since I had more important questions in mind—such as, "*Why* won't it be fun?"

"I will tell you later," replied Broxholm. "If I am able. Right now I have business to attend to."

His hands moved swiftly across the control board, which looked like a lot of marbles embedded in a sheet of black concrete. Sometimes he pushed the marbles (or whatever they were), sometimes he rolled them, sometimes he tapped them.

Suddenly a face appeared at the right of the panel. To my surprise, it didn't look like Broxholm. The forehead was low, the skull wide, the skin a strange shade of yellow.

"Oorbis tiktum?" asked the face.

"Broxholm, requesting emergency landing status. I have one young earthling with me."

I wondered why he spoke in English, until I remembered that his implant forced him to.

Clearly, the alien understood him anyway. "Coopla daktum!" cried the face. Its skin turned orange, and the screen went blank.

"He's not happy, is he?" I said.

"That was a she. And as I was supposed to arrive six hours later, with a total of five children, all of whom were supposed to be asleep, she is naturally somewhat disturbed."

By this time the docking beam had pulled us most of the way in. Imagine you're a flea. Now imagine you're walking through the door of the Empire State Building. That's what it was like for me going into the ship. For a while all I could think was, *This thing is so BIG!* Then my mind did a little flip, and I started thinking, *I'm so SMALL!*

Then I got sort of confused between being afraid and being excited.

Also, I had to go to the bathroom.

The docking beam pulled us into an area that had to be three times as long as a football field. The walls, which were about a thousand feet high, were lined with huge shelves. About half the shelf spaces were filled with spaceships.

None of the ships looked anything like Broxholm's.

When we were about three quarters of the way across this space, the docking beam deposited us on a shelf.

Broxholm did one of his nose-sighs. "Time to face the music," he said.

Given how much Broxholm hated music, that sounded worse coming from him than it would have from anyone else I had ever met. Or was it just his language implant, changing his words into a common English phrase?

I didn't have time to ask, because the top of the ship flipped up, and we began to float into the air. About a meter above the ship, we started to drift in different directions.

"Broxholm!" I cried. "What's going on?"

"We have to be disinfected," he answered, as a hole opened in the wall in front of me.

I struggled, but it was like fighting with air. No matter how I twisted, the invisible beam held me in its grip. Feet first, flat on my back, floating a hundred feet above the floor of the docking area, I was pulled into a small white room shaped a little like an egg that's been stood on end.

"Branna praxim pee-doongie prit," said a musical voice.

I looked around—which didn't take long, since the whole chamber wasn't more than four feet wide. I couldn't see whoever had spoken the words. I couldn't even see a device that the words might have come from.

"Branna praxim pee-doongie prit," repeated the voice gently.

A picture appeared on the wall. It showed an

alien—one who looked completely different from Broxholm—standing in a room like this. As I watched, the alien took off its clothes.

I blinked in surprise. Then I remembered the last thing Broxholm had said to me: "We have to be disinfected."

They wanted *me* to take off *my* clothes!

"Now just a ding-danged minute!" I said.

"Branna praxim pee-doongie prit," said the voice again.

"Uh-uh. Sorry. I don't do naked in front of strangers!"

Either whoever was speaking didn't understand me, or didn't care. A blue beam flashed down from the ceiling, locking me in place. It was a force field, just like the one Broxholm had used to keep Ms. Schwartz a prisoner. I tried to struggle, but I couldn't even scream. Everything stops when you're in a force field.

I heard the slightest of noises behind me. I tried to turn to see what had made it. I couldn't, of course. The force field held me firm.

Suddenly I felt something tickle down my back.

What was going on?

I heard the same noise in front of me. From the wall came a tiny ray of light. A laser beam! Starting at my chin, the laser moved all the way down to my feet. I couldn't see it all the way down, because I couldn't bend my head. But I could feel that tickle. A few more tickles—down my arms, around my legs, and suddenly the force field disappeared.

I could move again! The only problem was, the instant I did, my clothes all fell off. The laser had sliced my shirt, my pants, my shoes and socks, even my underwear, into pieces—and had done it all without touching my skin.

"Get me out of here!" I yelled. "Get me some *clothes*!"

No answer.

Did that mean there wasn't anyone there? Just as well, I decided, since I didn't have any clothes on. But how long were the aliens going to leave me here? Or was someone watching me even now—watching, but not speaking?

That made sense, in a way. If the alien mission was to study earthlings, then probably they were doing that right now—especially since I was the only one they had.

I decided if I was going to be *the* sample earthling, I was going to do my best not to act like an idiot. So I began to take deep breaths. I felt myself getting a little calmer. I mean, it wasn't like no one had ever seen me naked before. I've been to the doctor. And next year I would be taking showers in gym class.

Come to think of it, given my choice of getting stuck naked in front of a bunch of aliens, or in a seventh-grade gym class, I'd choose the aliens any day. At least *they* won't flick your butt with a wet towel!

Unfortunately, just as I was getting calm, my little chamber started to fill with gas. Was this a test, to see if I would panic? Were they going to knock me out and do some medical exams?

Or were they going to kill me and dissect me?

I held my breath until my lungs were screaming for air. When I couldn't resist any longer I took a deep, gasping breath.

"Prandit kooma," said the same voice I had heard before.

Weird musiclike sounds began drifting into the chamber. As I felt myself begin to get drowsy, I heard a slight hiss and saw a purple mist filtering down from the ceiling. I wanted to hold my breath again, but I didn't seem to have the will power.

The music played on. It wasn't like anything you or I would recognize as music, but it was beautiful. My eyelids drooped. Soon I slumped against the side of the chamber and slid to the floor, naked and sound asleep.

CHAPTER FOUR

CrocDoc

When I opened my eyes again, I was lying on a table in a room that was filled with soft green light. I was still naked. A tall alien who looked a little bit like a human crocodile—or at least like a human crocodile would look if it was red instead of green—was standing over me.

"Feeling better?" asked the alien softly.

Actually, what it said was, "Klaakah greebratz?" But my brain *heard* it as "Feeling better?"

I sat up, got dizzy, and laid back down.

"What's going on?" I whispered.

"I just did a little work on your head," said the alien, as casually as if it was announcing it had gone to the corner for a loaf of bread. "I'm sorry I didn't have a chance to explain the situation before I started, but I hadn't been expecting you."

"What did you do?" I asked, touching my head nervously.

"I installed a Universal Translator in your brain. That's why you can understand me. From now on, you'll be able to understand almost everyone you meet. We all wear them; it makes life quite a bit easier. As I said, I would have explained before I did the work, but there was no way to make you understand. The only being on board who had an implant that would turn his words *into* your language was Broxholm, and he was tied up."

Did the alien mean Broxholm was busy? Or had they really tied him up, as punishment for letting some kids mess up his mission? With aliens, who knew?

"You can probably sit up now," said the brain surgeon. "You just needed a moment to let your head clear."

Moving slowly, I pushed myself to a sitting position.

"Where are my glasses?" I asked.

"Do you need them?" asked the crocodile person, sounding surprised. (I would say the crocodile *man* or the crocodile *woman*, but the truth is, I had no idea which—if either—it was.)

I looked around and blinked in astonishment. I had never seen things so clearly in my life, not even when I was wearing glasses. "What happened?" I cried.

"I thought as long as I was poking around inside your head I might as well fix your eyes."

"Uh—thanks," I said. I probably should have been more enthusiastic; after all, the alien had done me a real favor. But I still wasn't comfort-

22

able with the idea that it had been poking around inside my skull without my permission.

On the other hand, being able to see so clearly without my glasses was *wonderful*!

"Thanks!" I said again, this time more sincere.

The red alien smiled—which meant that I got to see about three hundred and forty-two teeth—and said, "Don't mention it."

I heard a sound behind me. Turning, I saw another alien, though I couldn't spot the door he had come in by. He was short—probably not more than three feet tall—blue and bald. He had big eyes, a large nose, and a thick white mustache. He also had spindly arms and a potbelly. He was wearing nothing but a pair of baggy red shorts covered with pictures of jumping yellow fish.

I had seen aliens who were frightening, aliens who were strange, and aliens who were almost indescribable. This was the first one I had met who was *cute*.

"Greetings, Peter," said the newcomer. "My name is Hoo-Lan."

Actually, what he said was, "Grrgn ryxkzin, *Peter*, prrna-prrna Hoo-Lan." But with my new implant I knew exactly what he meant.

His ears flapped as he spoke. To my surprise, I understood that this was his version of a smile—which meant that my language implant translated not only words, but gestures and expressions. When you think about how much of what you mean is carried not by your words, but by your body, that makes sense. It's just not the kind of stuff they usually teach you in French class.

"How are you feeling?" he asked.

I thought about his question for a moment.

"I feel fine," I said finally.

The blue alien gave me another ear flap. "I'm pleased to hear that," he said, in his own language. "As you probably suspect, in addition to receiving a language implant, you have been disinfected. We had to disinfect both you and Broxholm before we could allow you to enter the main body of the ship. That was why he could not be with you when you had your operation, for which you have our apologies."

I was a little surprised to hear him apologize. It was also nice to know that the reason no one had told me what was going on when I first got here was that they just couldn't communicate with me yet.

"Can I stand up?" I asked, turning to the crocodile person.

"If you feel like it."

When I stopped to think about it, I realized that I felt terrific. Had the croc/doc tinkered with the rest of my systems, too? I decided not to ask.

"You wouldn't by any chance have some clothes I could wear, would you?" I asked.

Nose twitching, Hoo-Lan brought his hand from behind his back and tossed me a package wrapped in shiny black material. "I thought you might want these," he said. "Especially since it's time for us to visit the captain."

The package contained my clothes, which were in perfect condition. "I don't get it. I thought these had been lasered into pieces."

"These are computer recreations," said Hoo-Lan. "We put the disinfected scraps of what you had been wearing into the synthesizer. It analyzed fabric and design, then spit out a new set. These are identical to your originals, except that they are stain proof, and almost impossible to tear. If you wish, you can design your own clothes later."

That was interesting. I had never cared much about clothes. But if I could just tell the computer what I wanted, it might be fun to try a few different styles!

Once I was dressed I turned to the CrocDoc, as I now thought of him, and thanked him again for what he had done.

He tapped his elbows together three times. According to my implant, this meant he was glad to have been of service, and he hoped that he would never have to eat my children.

Let me tell you, this multicultural stuff can keep a guy on his toes!

"Follow me," said Hoo-Lan.

I nodded to CrocDoc, and got ready to follow Hoo-Lan out of the room. The only thing we needed now was a door.

The little alien walked to a place where the wall was marked by a large circle. Next to the circle were twelve rows of multicolored marbles. Hoo-Lan tapped six of the marbles, and the area inside the circle turned blue.

"Step through," he said, gesturing toward the circle.

"Through the wall?" I asked nervously.

"It's not a wall," he replied, giving me a little shove. "It's a transcendental elevator."

"Hey!" I shouted, thinking I was going to smash my face against the circle.

To my surprise, I stepped right *through* the circle. As I did, my whole body began to tingle. The tingling got stronger and stronger. It reminded me of the "pins and needles" you get when your leg falls asleep. Only this was all over my body, and it kept getting stronger.

I wanted to shout, only I couldn't, because I had no mouth. But then, I didn't have hands, feet, or a head, either.

CHAPTER FIVE

The Crystal Captain

As quickly as it began, it was over, and I found myself—all of myself—standing in a room that looked like it had been carved out of the inside of a diamond. Hoo-Lan was next to me.

"What happened?" I whispered.

Hoo-Lan looked at me in surprise. "Did you feel something?"

I nodded. He frowned, which meant the same for him as it does for us. "You shouldn't have," he said. "We'll have to look into this."

"But what happened?" I repeated.

"The elevator took you apart and put you back together."

"WHAT?"

"Don't worry—the same thing happened to me. That's how a transcendental elevator works; it breaks you into packets of energy, sends you to another place, then puts you back together."

"Wouldn't it be easier to walk?" I asked, patting myself in various places to make sure I was all there.

Hoo-Lan gave me his version of a shrug. "It's

over a hundred miles from the doctor's room to the captain's cabin."

"Oh, well in that case, sure, just send my molecules," I said, wondering if the sarcasm would translate.

"We did," said Hoo-Lan, sounding quite serious. "And now it is time for us to meet the captain."

A tinkle of music played around me. "Indeed it is," translated my language implant.

I turned in a circle, trying to find the source of the sound. "Where did that come from?" I whispered.

Hoo-Lan gestured to a clear tank that stood at one end of the chamber.

"What is it?" I asked.

"The captain."

"Come here, young earthling," said the tank.

I glanced at Hoo-Lan. He nodded, so I crossed to the tank, which looked like a huge, round aquarium. Except there weren't any fish or plants inside. A pair of cables ran from the bottom of the tank into the floor.

"Look more closely," said the voice.

I stared into the tank. After a few seconds I saw a collection of crystals, sharp-edged and many-faceted. It took me a few more seconds to realize that the shapes were slowly moving.

"This is our captain," said Hoo-Lan, adding a name for which there was no translation.

"But how . . . ?"

A sigh tinkled around me. "You carbon-based life forms are so molecular-centric. Until you meet another form of life, you seem convinced that carbon is the only way to grow."

"Sorry," I said. "I didn't mean to offend you."

The air around me filled with a sound like chimes; the implant told me this was laughter.

"Hoo-Lan," sang the crystal captain, "I need only speak to Peter. You may leave if you wish."

"I have things to do," said Hoo-Lan, nodding to me. "I will see you soon." As he turned and headed for the transcendental elevator the captain's voice said, "You do realize, my young friend, that you have created a problem for us?"

I blinked. "What's the problem?"

"In a word, *you*. By galactic law, no person of Earth is allowed on board this vessel."

"I thought Broxholm was supposed to bring back *five* of us," I said, feeling somewhat puzzled.

"For observation and analysis only. Any memory of the experience would have been erased from your minds before we returned you to Earth."

"Did you ever wonder how we might feel about that?"

"Not particularly. If I had, it wouldn't have mattered. Except for our fact-finding mission, the Interplanetary Council has banned all contact with the people of Earth. This is the first time in a thousand years this has happened, by the way."

"You mean it's the first time in a thousand years Earth has been isolated?" I asked, wondering if the aliens had visited a lot in the past.

"It's the first time in a thousand years *any* planet has been isolated."

I didn't like the sound of that. "Should we be honored?" I asked, sounding more smart-alecky than I intended.

"*Terrified* might be more appropriate."

"Terrified?" I squeaked. The very fact that the captain *said* I should react that way came close to creating the feeling in me.

The captain's voice chimed around me, louder than before. "Earth is the greatest danger faced in the three thousand year history of the Interplanetary League. It appears to be a planet in the grip of mass insanity. We must find out why you kill each other with such reckless abandon."

The language implant was translating what the captain sang into words. But the very sound of the music filled me with fear, and with sorrow.

The crystals in the bottom of the tank shifted. "There is something very strange about your world," continued the captain. "On every other planet where science has developed, the process has taken much longer than it has on Earth. Always before, people ready to enter space have been civilized in a way you humans have avoided altogether."

The captain paused, then sang sadly, "We fear if

the people of Earth are allowed into space in their uncivilized state, the results could be disastrous beyond anything you can imagine."

"Allowed?" I asked nervously.

"Allowed. At the moment, we are considering a permanent quarantine on Earth. No one gets on, no one gets off. We don't mind you exploring your own solar system; there's not much there anyway. But we cannot allow you to carry this sickness, whatever it is, into the galaxy at large."

I wanted to cry; for years I had been dreaming of meeting people from another planet. When I finally do meet some, what do I find? *My* planet has embarrassed itself in front of the entire galaxy! I felt like an interstellar geek.

"Of course, quarantine is only one option," said the captain, interrupting my thoughts.

"What else is there?" I asked, more nervous than ever.

"I would rather not say. After all, the teacher does not necessarily discuss all options with the student."

I wondered if the captain really meant "with the enemy." But I couldn't think of a way to say it that didn't sound snotty.

"Anyway," continued the captain, "you can see that your presence here creates a problem."

"Are you going to lock me up?"

The bells that filled the air seemed to sigh. "You see? Only an earthling would think of something

32

like that so quickly. I suppose if you persisted in causing trouble, we might lock you up. But that's just not something we do. However, we do have to decide what we *will* do with you. So tell me, what is it that brought you here? What do you want?"

"To *learn*," I said fiercely.

"Admirable. However, you must realize that the more you learn, the less likely it is we can ever let you return home."

"I don't care about home. I want to see the stars."

"You could have seen them from your own backyard."

"I want to visit other planets. I want to explore the galaxy. I want to find out what it's all about!" I cried, suddenly realizing I might be the only human *ever* to have that chance.

"Then you are welcome to join us. You will be assigned to Hoo-Lan, who has been specializing in Earth studies of late."

"How is Broxholm going to feel about that?" I asked, though for all I knew Broxholm never wanted to see me again.

"That's not an issue," said the captain. "Broxholm has other matters to which he must attend. As do I, my new crewmember. Which means that you must leave now. The elevator will take you to your cabin."

Feeling a trifle nervous, I headed for the circle

where we had come in. When I glanced back, the captain's tank had changed color. I heard the word for "Farewell" chime through the air as I stepped through the wall.

I didn't feel anything this time, none of the tearing sensation that had scared me so much on my first trip through the transcendental elevator. So I figured Hoo-Lan had adjusted the mechanism for me. But the place the elevator delivered me to was so dark I was afraid the thing had malfunctioned.

My heart began to pound. What if it had sent me someplace where no one would be able to find me, some neglected storage space or something? Rooms on this ship didn't even have doors! If I got stuck in a place like that I might die before anyone found me.

I was about to scream for help when a blue light began to glow behind me.

CHAPTER SIX

Hoo-Lan

I spun around and found myself face to face with Hoo-Lan.

Well, face to face isn't quite right; given how short he was, it was more like navel to face. Anyway, he was the source of the light. And I mean that exactly. The little alien wasn't carrying a lamp or a flashlight or anything. *He* was glowing—a soft, gentle glow that seemed to come from every square inch of his skin.

"For heaven's sakes, Peter," said Hoo-Lan quietly, "don't be so skittish."

It took me a moment to realize that the words were spoken in perfect English. I stared at him in surprise. "I didn't know you could speak my language."

"There's a lot about me that you don't know, and a great deal that I have to tell you. That's why I arranged to have you sent here, instead of your own room. I needed a place where we could speak in relative secrecy."

"Secrecy?" I asked nervously.

"Great things are happening," said Hoo-Lan,

glancing from side to side. "Power is shifting, and ancient mysteries are being unraveled." His glow seemed to grow more intense. His voice, and his words, sent a chill down my spine.

"What does that have to do with me?" I asked in a whisper.

"Nothing, and everything. Remember, information travels fast, if you know how to grease its skids." He paused, then added, "I'm not sure that made sense."

"Why are we here?" I asked, trying to get him back on track. "*Where* are we, for that matter?"

"In a storage space in the lower third of the good ship *New Jersey*, which at the moment is heading past the planet you call Jupiter."

That scared me. The last spacecraft Earth sent past Jupiter had taken years to get there. We must be moving at an incredible rate! On the other hand, it was a straight answer. Shooting for two in a row, I asked, "What did you bring me here to tell me?"

Hoo-Lan motioned toward a box, indicating I should sit. In the light emanating from his body, I could see that the room was filled with containers of all shapes, sizes, and colors.

I sat. Hoo-Lan scrambled up next to me. Reaching into a pocket in his baggy shorts, he pulled out a black box about half the size of a paperback book.

"You rat," he said, handing it to me.

"What did I do?" I asked, feeling hurt.

Hoo-Lan blinked. "What did you . . . ? Oh, you misunderstood me. I didn't call *you* a rat. *This device* is a URAT—a *U*niversal *R*eader *A*nd *T*ranslator. Press your thumb against the top corner."

I did as Hoo-Lan said. The box opened, pretty much the way a book would if it was only made of two very thick pages. Except the URAT was now stiff, as if it had never been closed.

"This will be your primary information source," said Hoo-Lan. "It contains a small library of important data for navigating your way around the ship. Also a complete listing of crew members. Now, please tell it your name."

"My name is—"

"Wait, wait! I think you need a new name."

"What's wrong with the one I've got?" I asked, feeling a little annoyed. I don't know why I was annoyed. Peter Thompson was nothing special as names go. Heck, the Thompson part came from my father, and I was as glad to be rid of him as he was to be rid of me. No loss there. As for my first name, it was mostly something people used to get my attention when they wanted to tease me. So a new name shouldn't have been any big deal. Still, I had had this one all my life, and I felt somewhat attached to it.

"There's nothing *wrong* with your old name," said Hoo-Lan patiently. "It's just that it's part of your old life. New life, new name, I always say. I shall call you Krepta, which in the language of my world means 'Child of the Stars.' This is a good name for you, since you are a boy without a planet."

I felt my stomach twist. "A boy without a planet" sounded terribly lonely.

I hesitated. "My name is Krepta," I whispered into the URAT. "Child of the Stars."

"Greetings, Krepta," replied the URAT. "How may I be of service?"

I looked at Hoo-Lan.

"Tell it you wish to travel," he said.

"Where do you wish to go?" asked the URAT, after I had followed Hoo-Lan's advice.

"Actually, I would like something to eat," I said.

"Wise choice," said Hoo-Lan. "Biologically sound, too. When you get to a new place, always find out where to eat and where to hide."

"Will I need to hide here?" I asked nervously.

Hoo-Lan shrugged. I would have pursued the question, but the URAT had started beeping. Looking at it, I saw a pattern of colored dots. It was the same pattern I had seen next to the transcendental elevator. Suddenly some of the dots began to flash.

"It's displaying the destination code," said Hoo-Lan. "When you want to go somewhere, ask the URAT for the code. Punch the code into the control pad beside any elevator, and it will take you to your destination."

"Can I go anywhere I want?"

"Of course," said Hoo-Lan. "Why not?"

"Well, don't you have rules—you know, security precautions against spies, things like that?"

"You have to stop thinking as if you were still on Earth, Peter. We're not the same as you are. I'm the closest thing to a spy on this ship. Certainly the biggest troublemaker."

I looked at him in alarm. "Are you going to get *me* in trouble?" I asked nervously.

"Oh, probably. Anyone who tries to do something worthwhile gets in trouble now and then, don't you think?"

To tell you the truth, I didn't know what to think. I decided to get some more information, and do the thinking later. "What do you mean, you're the closest thing to a spy?" I asked. "Are you a spy, or aren't you?"

"Merely a representative of a minority point of view. As you know, your planet is currently the focus of a great debate. At the moment, I am on the losing side of that debate."

"What side is that?"

Before Hoo-Lan could answer, I heard another beeping. Reaching into his pocket, he took out a second URAT. When he opened it, a face that looked like it belonged to a purple frog appeared on its surface and said, "You are wanted for an urgent meeting."

"The main problem with these things," said Hoo-Lan, tucking away his URAT and hopping down to the floor, "is that they're great for communication, but lousy for privacy. I'm sorry, Krepta, but I can't ignore this call. We'll talk more later. For now, why don't you get something to eat. I'll catch up with you in a while."

He crossed to the wall and started to punch a code into the elevator buttons. Then he stopped, turned to me, and said, "Since you can't see in the dark, maybe you'd better go first."

That made sense. When Hoo-Lan left he would take my only source of light—namely, himself—with him.

I stepped up to the wall. My URAT was still flashing the code for a dining area, the image of the buttons lighting up in a certain order, pausing, and then repeating the sequence.

I watched the code twice, then punched it into the control pad. Taking a deep breath, I stepped through the wall—and into the middle of a fight.

CHAPTER SEVEN

Lunch with Fleef and Gurk

"It was a bad idea from the beginning!" said an alien who looked something like a tall brown pickle with arms.

"Nonsense!" snapped the orange alien standing next to him. "A few hours wouldn't have made the slightest bit of difference to those creatures."

This second alien was only a little taller than me, and clearly female, at least by Earth standards. Though her skin was orange, her features were basically human—well, except for the fact that she had a thumb-thick green stalk rising from the top of her head. The stalk ended in a thick knob, which I took to be a sense organ of some sort, since it was constantly rotating. Every once in a while it would stop moving and go, "Neep! Neep!"

"Ah, look!" cried the orange alien, when she noticed me standing there. "We can ask him!"

"It might be nice if we greeted him first," said the pickle.

"Flog me for an oaf!" cried the orange one. "I just get too excited sometimes." Turning to me, she said, "You are the Earth child, are you not?"

Her voice was sweet and gentle.

"I used to be," I replied. "Now I'm a child of the stars."

The orange alien nudged the pickle. "What did I tell you, Gurk. It doesn't matter!"

Gurk squeezed one of the warty things that covered his pickly skin. It popped, releasing a terrible smell.

My implant told me this was his way of saying "Nonsense!"

"Euuuw!" cried the orange alien. "I told you not to do that!" The stalk on the top of her head flopped backwards. "Neep," it whispered. "Neee—"

I looked at the alien in alarm, worried that the knob might be permanently disabled, or even dead. But she seemed more annoyed than concerned.

Gurk put his hands on top of his head, which was a gesture of apology. "Sorry, I got carried away. But I still think you're mistaken. Let's start this conversation over, or we'll give the young one a bad impression."

He turned to me. I got ready to hold my breath, in case he was going to communicate by smell again. But his voice was quiet, and when I looked at him more carefully, I realized that he had the kindest, warmest eyes I had ever seen.

42

Putting his skinny arms together in front of him, he said, "Young one, my name is Gurk. My companion is called Fleef."

"Greetings," said Fleef, who was trying to get the stalk on her head to stand up again.

"Greetings," I replied.

They both looked at me expectantly. "And *your* name?" asked Gurk, after a moment of silence.

"Oh, I'm sorry. My name is—" I hesitated. Was I Peter Thompson—or was I Krepta?

The aliens were staring at me. I had a sense that they were beginning to wonder if I was stupid.

"My name is Krepta!" I said defiantly.

As I said it, I felt something twist inside me. I had let go of my name and my home, and though I had a new name, and a new home, neither one of them felt like they were really mine.

I wondered if they ever would. I almost said, "Wait, I made a mistake! My name is Peter!"

But that would have been a lie. I wasn't Peter anymore. Hoo-Lan had been right. I was a boy without a planet, and the name I had carried away from Earth no longer fit me.

"Krepta!" said Gurk in surprise. "A Child of the Stars, indeed. And what happened to the name you were born with?"

"I am a different person now," I said softly.

"Well, Krepta," said Fleef, "come and sit with

us while we eat. Perhaps you can help us settle a disagreement."

I wasn't sure I wanted to eat with the two of them. Still, if I was going to get along on this ship, I did need to start making friends.

"I'd be glad to eat with you," I said, hoping neither one of them was going to eat something so gross I would get sick just watching them swallow it.

"Are you touchable?" asked Gurk.

I raised an eyebrow. His translator must have interpreted the movement, because he answered the question before I could put it into words.

"Some beings like to be touched, others are deeply offended by certain kinds of contact," he explained, his wonderful eyes looking straight into mine. "If touch does not bother you, then I would put my arm around your shoulder, or place a hand on the back of your neck, to guide you to the sitting place. But it is best to ask, first."

I hesitated. My father wasn't much of a hugger. So the only person who had touched me much back home was Duncan Dougal, and that was only to punch me. Since I wasn't used to it, I was a little nervous about having Gurk touch me, especially with that pickly skin of his. On the other hand, this was a new world, a new life. . . .

"It's okay," I said. "You can touch me."

I thought about adding something about being careful *where* he touched me, but he had been so worried about offending me at all, I decided it wasn't going to be a problem.

Besides, even though I hadn't gone three steps past the elevator, I could see a whole room full of people just beyond Fleef and Gurk. So I figured I was safe for the time being—at least, as safe as a kid can be in a room where he's the only person who looks more than vaguely human.

Taking me by the arm, Gurk led me to a table at the edge of the room. "There are many beings interested in you," he whispered, "so there's no need to draw too much attention to yourself right now."

"For once we agree," said Fleef.

"Neep!" said the thing on top of her head. I noticed the stalk was standing up straight again.

I also noticed that the room was sort of dim. I was a little puzzled about this, until I decided they had probably set the light at a level most comfortable for the greatest number of different beings.

"Where do we get our food?" I asked.

"Right here!" said Fleef, gesturing to the table.

The table was round, with a smooth black top. In front of each of us was a set of buttons much like the ones beside the transcendental elevators.

"Do we use these to order?" I asked, pointing to the buttons.

"See, I told you they weren't stupid!" said Gurk.

"Intelligence and emotion are not always connected," replied Fleef. Her orange skin grew darker as she spoke, which my translator informed me was a sign that she was irritated.

"Could you tell me what this is all about?" I asked, trying not to do anything that was going to offend either one of them.

"Later," said Gurk. "First let's order. Have you programmed in any meals yet?"

I shook my head, trusting Gurk's implant to translate the gesture.

"All right, then we'll have to show you how. You are a carbon-based life form, if I remember correctly?"

I nodded, wondering what they would feed me if I wasn't.

"All right, first you punch in your personal code—"

"But I don't have a personal code," I interrupted.

"Gurk," said Fleef gently, "let *me* show him how."

Gurk slid some warts around, which was his way of sighing, and sat back in his chair while Fleef showed me how to find my personal code. Then she helped me tell the master computer the kinds of things that I would like. It took a while, because the food synthesizer wasn't programmed for an earthling. But by asking careful questions, she was able to help me come up with a menu

that we both felt would (a) not kill me and (b) not make me throw up.

We all punched in the codes for our meals at the same time. Within seconds a hole opened in the top of the table. Three plates floated out and positioned themselves in front of us.

Gurk's plate had a steaming, writhing mess of something that looked like it wanted to crawl across the table and say hello to me.

Fleef's dinner looked like blue marbles and smelled like rotten eggs mixed with toe jam.

The stuff on my plate actually looked pretty good. That was because Fleef had showed me how to program color and shape into my order. While it didn't taste quite as good as it looked, at least most of it was edible. The only thing I couldn't get down was the stuff that looked like french fries but tasted like peanut butter mixed with rotten blueberries.

While we ate, Fleef told me how to refine my next order, based on what I did and didn't like in this batch of stuff. She was a good teacher, and I was starting to like her.

After we had all had a bit to eat, Gurk said, "Here's the question we were arguing about when you stepped out of the elevator. What would happen if—"

Before he could finish, the lights blinked three times. "Better lie down, Krepta," said Fleef, throwing herself to the floor. "You'll be less likely to throw up that way."

CHAPTER EIGHT

Faster Than Light

I stretched out on the floor beside Fleef and Gurk. After a second, I raised my head. Almost everyone else in the large room was on the floor with us.

"Put your head down," whispered Fleef. "Quickly!"

I felt like I was in one of those stories where the king was about to come by, and everyone had to bow down. I stared at the ceiling, wondering if the aliens had some supreme high commander they treated like a god.

At first, I thought the ceiling was made of green marble. Then I noticed that the swirls of color were slowly moving. I was thinking how pretty it was when an ear-splitting squeal sliced through the room, as if some monstrous claw had just scraped across the blackboard of the universe. A low moan rose from the aliens on the floor, the kind of sound you might hear if a thousand kids all began to feel carsick at the same time.

It took me a moment to realize that my own voice was part of that mass moan. My stomach lurched. I clutched at it, trying to keep down what I had eaten. I didn't want to disgust my new friends by throwing up on them! (I was also hoping they were not going to throw up on me. I was pretty nervous about what it might smell like if Gurk tossed his cookies—or whatever it is that giant pickles toss when they lose their lunches.)

Suddenly I felt like I was being pulled apart. Only this was a thousand times worse than my first trip through the transcendental elevator. It was as if some giant had my head, another had my feet, and they were having a tug of war—with about a thousand other people pulling at the top, bottom, and sides of me just for the heck of it.

About the time I thought I absolutely couldn't stand it any longer, it stopped. I lay flat for a moment, wondering what had just happened to me.

Gurk touched my shoulder. "Are you all right, Krepta?" he asked softly.

I was so disoriented it took me a moment to realize he was speaking to me. "I'm not sure," I whispered. "What just happened?"

"The ship made a space-shift," said Fleef softly. "Galactically speaking, it's the only way to travel."

I opened and closed my eyes a few times. The ceiling didn't seem so pretty anymore. In fact, it was kind of nauseating. I wished it would stop moving.

"What's a space-shift?" I asked weakly.

"Instant transportation," said Gurk, rolling over and pushing himself up with his skinny arms.

"Like the transcendental elevators, but on a grand scale," added Fleef. She was already on her feet, holding out a six-fingered orange hand to help me up. "The ship just moved several light-years from where it was when you joined us."

I felt an unexpected sense of loss wash over me. How far from home was I now?

"Could you tell me a bit more?" I asked.

"Well, do you know about the speed of light?" asked Gurk.

"It goes 186,000 miles per second," I said, trusting their implants to figure out what miles are. "It's the fastest thing we know."

"It's the fastest thing *anyone* knows," said Fleef, patting her stalk to make sure it was all right. "Now that would make traveling around the galaxy nearly impossible, since even at the speed of light it would take you years to get from one star system to another. Centuries, sometimes."

"So the best method is to skip all that traveling," said Gurk, sliding a wart across his forehead. "Which is what we just did."

I staggered to my chair, trying to keep my stomach from providing a review of everything I had just eaten. "Could you make that a little more clear?"

Gurk punched some buttons on the food preparation device. A plate floated up, carrying a thick red noodle that had to be at least three feet long. "How can you eat so soon after that shift?" asked Fleef.

"This isn't a snack, it's a demonstration," replied Gurk. "Sit down, Krepta, and I will try to explain." He picked up the noodle. "If you stretch out this *bee-ranga*—which, by the way, is the preferred snack on the planet Hopfner— you have a straight line. Now, if you were at one end, and the place you wanted to go was at the other end, you would have to travel the entire length of the *bee-ranga* to get there, right?"

I nodded.

"But if you join the ends of the *bee-ranga*, like this, all you would have to do is go from here— to here!" And with that he brought the two ends of the noodle together.

"What does that have to do with us?" I asked.

"That's how this ship travels. We bring two parts of space together and then step across them."

"It's the stepping across that's the hard part," added Fleef. "It makes most beings quite queasy."

"But how do you *do* it?"

"I don't know how it works," said Gurk. "All I know is the basic idea."

That seemed strange, until I thought about how many people on Earth ride around in cars without having the slightest idea of how they work. I decided to switch questions. "If we just jumped several light-years, then where are we now?"

"How do you expect us to know?" asked Gurk, popping the *bee-ranga* into his mouth. "We're not the captain."

The sight of Gurk eating seemed to make Fleef queasy. "If my friend were feeling a little more polite," she whispered, "he would mention that you could find out by asking your URAT. I would guess we're heading back toward the center of the galaxy. If that was a typical jump, we probably moved about twenty light-years."

A strange feeling came over me. *The fastest rocket ever built on earth couldn't get this far in a hundred years*, I thought to myself.

With a shock, I realized I was homesick.

Fleef tapped me on the shoulder. "Are you all right, Krepta?"

"What? Oh, sure," I lied. "I'm fine, just fine."

I figured there was no point in telling them how I felt. To begin with, I wasn't sure I understood it myself. Besides, years of living with my father had taught me not to bother talking about things that upset me.

"Good," said Fleef. "Then maybe I can finally ask you my question. What we were arguing about when you first met us was whether or not it made any difference if we borrowed some of your planet's children for a while."

"You mean like when Broxholm was planning to steal some kids from our school?" I asked.

"No, no, no," said Fleef. "We weren't going to steal anyone—just borrow them for a while. It's part of a research project. We would have brought them back! Which is why I don't think anyone would have minded that much. But Gurk says people, parents especially, would have been terribly upset. So—which of us is right?"

"Gurk is. Parents would have gone berserk. You can't just go around stealing—er, *borrowing* kids like that."

"See!" said Gurk triumphantly. Actually, he didn't say it, he pulled off one of his brown warts and waved it in front of Fleef's face, which my translation device told me was a sign of victory.

"But it doesn't make sense," said Fleef. She looked upset. Not just unhappy because Gurk had won the argument; she seemed genuinely disturbed.

"What doesn't make sense?" I asked.

"Oh, ignore her," said Gurk. "She's just annoyed because she wants to believe you people don't have well developed emotions."

"Why would you want to believe that?" I asked.

Fleef didn't answer. Gurk spoke for her. "Because then she won't feel so bad if we have to blow up your planet."

CHAPTER NINE

Room Service

If you've ever just missed being in some terrible car accident, you know what I felt like. My hands were trembling, my heart was pounding, and my stomach wasn't sure where it wanted to go.

"You want to do what?" I whispered, staring at Fleef in horror.

The stalk on her head was whirling around like crazy, the little knob going "Neep neep neep!" as if someone was trying to catch and kill it. According to my implant this was a sign of extreme emotional distress.

Tough! I thought. *Your distress can't be any worse than mine.*

Sure, I'd had my problems with Earth. But these guys were talking about blowing up billions of human beings, including my father, Ms. Schwartz, Susan Simmons—and *you.*

"You'd better go, Krepta," said Gurk, touching my arm.

"No! I want to know what this is all about."

Gurk rearranged a few warts, a signal that the

topic was definitely closed. I decided leaving was a good idea after all. If I wasn't going to get any more information, I needed some time and some privacy to think about what I had just heard.

As I pushed myself away from the table, Fleef reached out and touched my arm. "Please do not take this personally, Krepta. We will discuss it more later."

I looked at her in astonishment. "You want to blow up my planet, and I'm not supposed to take it personally?" I asked.

Shaking with fury, I stalked away from the table.

At the transcendental elevator I asked the URAT to give me the code for my room. At once a pattern flashed on the screen. I punched it into the keypad, stepped through the elevator, and found myself in an egg-shaped space. Its curving wall was a soft brownish-orange color. Since there were no doors or windows, it really felt like being inside an egg.

I liked the color and the shape of the room. Unfortunately, it was completely bare, with not a stick of furniture to be seen.

Broxholm's house had been bare of furniture, too. Was that the alien style? Did they expect me to just sit on the floor, staring at the walls?

It's interesting how much little things can distract you when you have something big on your mind. What I wanted to do was worry about the fate of the Earth. What I found myself fretting about was the fact that I didn't have a chair to sit and worry in.

I decided to ask the URAT. Flipping open the box, I said "Can I have some furniture?"

"Certainly," replied the mechanical voice.

"Well, how do I get it?"

"All you need to do is ask."

"I'm asking."

"You have to specify what you want."

"What kind of choices do I have?" I asked, trying not to sound too impatient.

"We have an enormous variety of personal convenience items on file," said the URAT. "You can also design your own. The possibilities are infinite."

"Is there a way to know what you have on file?"

Instantly the wall in front of me began to display a picture. That was neat; the entire wall was like a giant television screen—except that the image was clearer than any television you have ever seen.

The picture it showed now was actually a chart, with all kinds of furniture on it—and I do mean all kinds. Not only did it show chairs, desks, and beds, it had items that looked like everything from medieval torture devices to toilets designed for octopi.

Which reminded me: "Is there a bathroom attached to this room?"

"No."

"Then how am I supposed to go to the toilet?" I cried, suddenly feeling desperate.

"There are many bathrooms available, simply none attached to this room, Krepta."

That made sense. After all, if a transcendental elevator could move you from one place to another instantly, there was no need to have your bathroom actually *attached* to your room. It could be fifty miles away, and it wouldn't make any difference. Maybe you didn't even *have* your own bathroom; for all I knew, the elevator just sent you to the first empty bathroom it found.

"Give me the code for a bathroom, please," I said to the URAT.

"Insufficient data."

"What do you mean?" I cried, crossing my legs.

"I do not know what kind of bathroom you need. We have fifty-three different types of facilities."

I remembered the octopi toilets, or whatever they were, that I had seen on the first chart. Given the variety of aliens I had met already, it made sense that the ship needed a lot of different bathrooms.

"I'm glad I'm not the plumber for this place," I muttered.

"Yes," agreed the URAT, "that would be a disaster."

"Look, I don't need to be insulted by a machine. Just tell me how to find a bathroom!"

The URAT informed me that it needed to know more about me. After it had asked fifteen or twenty questions, some of them very personal, it finally gave me a bathroom code.

Not a moment too soon! I thought, as I punched the code into the control pad. I stepped into a bathroom that was only mildly odd— which is to say that it only took me about five minutes (five desperate minutes) to figure out how to use it.

When I was done, I returned to my own room. The furniture chart was still on the wall. I wondered if it only showed available *categories* of furniture, since there was only one chair, one desk, one octopus's toilet, and so on.

"Can you show me other chairs?" I asked.

Instantly, the image changed to a chart that held over fifty different kinds of chairs.

"Can I have one of those?" I asked, pointing to a comfortable looking armchair.

"Color?" asked the URAT.

"What do you have?"

A chart with about a hundred colors appeared on the wall. After I chose one I liked, the URAT asked about size.

Size? Chairs are chairs, right?

Not when you're on a ship the size of New Jersey, filled with who knows how many varieties of aliens.

By the time I was done answering questions, we had designed a chair that was as perfectly matched to me as a handmade suit would have been. This was neat!

What was even neater was that after I finally gave the URAT all the information it requested I heard a humming noise. Less than five minutes later the very chair I had ordered popped through the door of the transcendental elevator.

This was the ultimate in home shopping!

Plunking down in my chair, I tried to think. From what Fleef and Gurk had said, while some aliens wanted to blow up the Earth, no definite decision had been made yet.

Even so, it was clear that the planet was in danger. Only I got the feeling that since I had abandoned Earth, no one expected me to care.

But I did care. Earth was in danger. I was the only one who could save it. And I didn't have the first idea how to begin.

Suddenly I felt very small, and very frightened.

I held out my hands and stared at them. They weren't big enough to hold the fate of the world.

CHAPTER TEN

The Alien Council

After I sat for an hour or so without getting any ideas, I decided to look for Broxholm. Maybe he would help me.

Of course, for all I knew, he was one of the ones in favor of torching the planet.

But somehow I couldn't bring myself to believe that.

The problem was, where to find him? The *New Jersey* had thousands, maybe millions of rooms. It seemed like an impossible task, until it occurred to me that given what I had seen so far, it was likely the ship had a way to keep track of folks.

So I asked the URAT where Broxholm was.

Within seconds, I had an elevator code. I punched a few buttons, stepped through the wall, and found myself staring at Broxholm's back. This put me in the minority; everyone else in the room was staring at Broxholm's front.

"Everyone else" consisted of a group of eight aliens arranged in a half circle. Some were sitting, some standing. One dangled from the ceiling in a sling. Another was stretched across a rack that held up its purple tentacles. At the top of the rack a nozzle released a lavender mist that kept the tentacles moist and gleaming.

"We expect to reconnect with Kreeblim soon," said the alien in the rack. "She should be able to rewire one of the earthlings so that—"

The alien broke off when it noticed me. Broxholm, realizing that the alien was looking past him, turned to see what was going on.

"Peter!" he said sharply. "What are you doing here?"

"Looking for you," I whispered. I was frightened; it was clear I had stumbled into a place where I didn't belong.

The knobs on Broxholm's head began to throb. "Return to your room," he ordered. "I will be there directly."

I nodded and turned to go. But before I could leave, the tallest of the aliens, a huge sea-green creature who towered over even Broxholm, said, "Wait. As long as the child is here, let's talk with him a bit."

He looked around the semicircle of aliens. They all made gestures of agreement, which in this case ranged from a simple nod to a triple armpit fart.

"Tell us why you are here," said the alien with purple tentacles.

I thought for a moment before I answered.

"Because I believe the human race was born to go to the stars," I said at last. "It's what I've dreamed of since I was old enough to understand the idea."

"Tell us about your school," said another alien.

I did as he asked. The aliens listened carefully, making gestures of agreement, or interest, or annoyance. Sometimes they seemed astonished—sometimes astonished and disgusted, as when I described our basal readers.

"That will be enough for now," said the sea-green alien suddenly. "Thank you for your time."

"Wait for me in your room," said Broxholm, as I walked past him back toward the elevator.

I nodded, and continued toward the wall.

When I got back to the room, I was shaking. I don't like talking in front of people. It makes me nervous.

I was using the URAT to get a better understanding of the ship when Broxholm reappeared.

I had started by trying to find out why the ship was so huge. I couldn't believe they had sent something this big halfway across the galaxy just to drop a few spies on Earth.

It turns out that the method the aliens use for skipping over huge distances requires a kind of gravity distortion that can only be achieved with an enormous ship. In fact, the *New Jersey* was actually the smallest starship yet built.

The reason the loading dock was half empty was that the *New Jersey* had been dropping off smaller vessels here and there as it wandered through the galaxy. That was actually its main job: shuttling between stars, leaving a ship, or a dozen, one place, picking up new ships in the next. That, and carrying out the orders of the Interplanetary Council.

I was so engrossed in what I was reading that I actually jumped and shouted when Broxholm came through the wall.

"What's wrong?" he cried in alarm.

"Nothing," I said. "You just startled me."

Broxholm made a sign of understanding. "I suppose anyone living on a planet as violent as yours would need that kind of reflex reaction to stay alive."

Even though I had chosen to leave Earth, I was a little sick of hearing it get dumped on like this. "And what were you and your pals discussing?" I asked bitterly. "Some nice, nonviolent way to blow up the planet?"

It was Broxholm's turn to look startled. But he took it in stride. "That *is* one option being considered," he said calmly.

My stomach twisted at his words. Out here, so far from home, it was easier to remember the good things about Earth—things like Susan Simmons, dolphins, and chocolate chip cookies.

"How can you even consider something like

that?" I asked, trying to fight back sudden, unexpected tears.

Broxholm gave his nose a pull. "I didn't say *I* was considering it. I said it was under consideration. Peter, you have to understand that the entire galaxy is in an uproar over this situation. We've been letting it ride for a while—we even got a break from making our decision because your planet's science got sidetracked a few decades ago. But the time is nearing when we must deal with what is known *across the stars* as 'The Earth Question.'"

"Why?"

"Because while they are not aware of it, your people are fast approaching the breakthrough point in space travel."

"You mean we're about to figure out how to go faster than light?" I whispered in awe.

Broxholm nodded. "We've been monitoring your science carefully. We know, better than you yourselves, how soon you will be able to come into space."

He paused, then crouched in front of me. Putting his hands on my shoulders, he looked directly into my eyes and said, "Do you understand what that means, Peter?"

I shook my head, feeling somewhat baffled.

"It means that for the first time in the 3,000 year history of the Interplanetary League, we are going to have to deal with a people who are at once smart enough to conquer space, and foolish enough to have wars. It means a peace that has lasted for 3,000 years, a peace that extends over 10,000 worlds, is in danger. Of course we are considering extreme measures. But the fate of Earth is by no means decided. The truth is, there are four main plans under consideration."

"What are they?" I asked, not entirely sure I wanted to know.

"One group believes we should take over your planet. A second thinks we should leave you on your own and see what happens; they believe you'll destroy yourselves before we ever have to worry about you. The third group wants to quarantine you—"

"What do you mean by 'quarantine'?" I interrupted.

"Cut you off from all connection with the greater galaxy," said Broxholm. "This could be done by setting up a space shield beyond which you could not pass, or by planting agents on Earth to sabotage your science, so that you could not learn how to get off the planet."

"That's terrible!" I cried, furious at the thought of anyone trying to bar us from space, from exploring the stars.

"I agree," said Broxholm. "But not as terrible as what might happen if you actually move into the galaxy at large. That is why one group simply wants to destroy the planet. They don't like the idea. But they think it is far better than letting you loose on the galaxy in your present condition."

"But why don't you just help us?" I cried, feeling scared and angry all at once.

Broxholm closed his orange eyes. "We don't know if we can. We believe there is something dangerously wrong with your people. This belief is based on three factors. First, the way you've treated your planet. Second, the incredible violence you do to each other. Third—and this is the really amazing thing to us—there's the condition of your brains."

"Our brains?"

Broxholm pulled on his nose, then let it snap back into place. "What baffles us most of all is the fact that the human race has the most powerful brain of any species in the galaxy."

CHAPTER ELEVEN

Anthropologists from Space

I stared at Broxholm for a moment, then whacked the side of my head as if I thought my hearing had gone bad. "Say that again?" I asked.

"You heard me," he replied. "The human race has what may be the most powerful brain in the galaxy." He tapped one green finger against my forehead. "Trapped inside that skull is a brain that is the envy of every being on this ship."

"But I'm not smarter than the people here," I said—which was hard for me to admit, since being smart was the one thing I had always taken pride in. I paused, then added, "Am I?"

Broxholm shook his head. "No, you're not. But you *could* be. That's part of the mystery. The human brain is not only the most amazing piece of organic matter in the galaxy; it is also the *least used* brain in the known universe. We've never encountered anything like it—nowhere seen such a gap between what *could* be and what *is*."

As he talked, I began to get the feeling that Broxholm was actually jealous of the human brain.

"Do you have any idea what the rest of us

could have accomplished if we had your brain?" he asked feverishly. "Any idea how it galls us to see that potential, and know how little you have done with it?"

I shook my head, too amazed to say a word.

"What terrifies us is what might happen if you learn to use your full intelligence *before* you become truly civilized. Stars above! If you people find your way into space before you fix whatever's wrong with your spirits, the damage you'd wreak could make what you've done to your own planet look like a forest rangers' picnic."

I sat back against the wall, staring at him. What could I say?

"Why do you think I was on your planet?" continued Broxholm. "What do you think was the point of trying to bring some of you back here for short-term study? We're trying to figure out why you act the way you do. We're looking for an answer—a cure, if you want to call it that."

He was pacing the floor now, not really angry, but agitated. It turned out that he had studied for years to make the trip to Earth. He was one of a group of aliens you might call "Anthropologists from Space"—a team watching the whole human race as if it was a tribe in the jungle.

A new question struck me. "If you guys are so wonderful, why were *you* so mean to our class?" I asked, remembering the way he had acted as a teacher.

Broxholm tugged on his nose. "For one thing, I am naturally gruff. Secondly, I would point out that you earthlings have a funny idea of what constitutes 'mean.' On my world we don't worry nearly so much as you people do about talking nicely to each other. We speak the truth and get on with things. On the other hand, we don't leave people to starve in the streets."

He paused, then added, "Actually, my natural gruffness was *not* the reason I behaved as I did with your class. I could easily have been as sweet and kind as anyone might have wished. However we were making a study of your learning styles—how you respond to different methods of education. We have an agent working in your town right now who is as 'nice' as I was nasty. It's all part of our study."

"You mean you're not really a creep?" I asked.

Broxholm stared at me. For a moment I was afraid he was going to be angry. But suddenly his nose began to twitch, just a little at first, then faster and harder, as if something inside was struggling to get out.

I realized that if he was an earthling, he would have been roaring with laughter.

"Peter," he said, "where I come from, I'm considered to be what you would call 'a real pussycat.' Look, young one, what was your greatest desire in all the world?"

"To see the stars!" I said, though suddenly I realized that my heart was saying something else.

I pushed the thought away. It was too frightening.

"To see the stars," said Broxholm. "Don't you think I knew that? Do you have any idea what trouble I caused myself by bringing you here?"

I shook my head.

He paused. "Nor need you know," he said at last. "Other than to understand that I chose to ignore a powerful command for two reasons. The first was that I owed you a favor for helping me escape *without having to hurt anyone.*"

I shivered as I realized just what Broxholm meant by that. "What was the second reason?" I whispered.

He spread his hands. "I like you," he said.

I blinked. Why was I starting to cry?

"Thank you," I whispered, feeling really stupid.

Broxholm put his arms around me. "You poor boy," he whispered. Then he stood and turned away. "Oh, you poor people," he said, so softly that I could barely hear him. "You poor, sad, wonderful people, so full of love and hate, hope and horror, sorrow and need."

He made a terrible, rasping sound, and suddenly I realized that he was weeping. Weeping for a planet that wasn't his, and all the pain that he had seen there.

I ran to him, threw my arms around him.

Then the two of us stood in the center of my room, and cried until we had no tears left.

CHAPTER TWELVE

How to Use a URAT

So that was my first day on board the *New Jersey*. Is it any wonder I was exhausted?

Now you may have noticed that my "day" had started at night. But time on the ship was not related to time on Earth—or more specifically, time in Kennituck Falls. The ship had its own rhythm, and while there were times when more of its inhabitants were resting than others, in general it was busy twenty-seven hours a day.

According to Hoo-Lan, days on the ship were twenty-seven hours long because that was the schedule that made the most sense for the greatest number of beings on board.

Of course, since it was easy to control light and temperature, many of the aliens had private spaces to suit their personal needs. In some chambers the days were only ten hours long, and the temperature was like Death Valley during a heat wave. Some had long hot days, others had short cold days, and so on. Even so, everyone was able to function in the ship's main area—though it did mean that some of them had to wear thick layers of clothing, while others were nearly naked.

After Broxholm left that first "night," I used the URAT to get myself something to sleep in. The most interesting thing on the chart—at least, the most interesting thing that looked like I could actually sleep in it—was a kind of hammock device. The only problem was, I couldn't figure out where to hang it, since the walls in my room were smooth, and I had a feeling I wasn't supposed to put screws or nails in them, even if I had screws or nails, which I didn't.

I should have known not to worry. Each end of the hammock had a rope. At the end of the rope was a ball. When you threw the ball at the ceiling, it stuck wherever it struck, and didn't come down until you gave the rope three sharp tugs.

So I got myself a hammock and hung it from my ceiling.

It was like sleeping on a cloud—though by the time I got it hung up, I was so exhausted I probably could have slept on a bed of cold seaweed and hot rocks.

I had no clock, so I don't know how long I had been asleep when I was awakened by a sudden loud buzzing.

"Who—what?" I sputtered. I tried to get up, but only succeeded in rocking the hammock sideways.

"It's not Hoo-Wat, it's Hoo-Lan," said an offended-sounding voice that seemed to come from nowhere. "May I come in?"

"I suppose so," I yawned, too groggy to think of just telling him to go away.

Almost instantly Hoo-Lan came walking through my wall. His blue shorts were covered with purple, red, and yellow flowers so bright that if I had still been asleep they probably would have woken me all by themselves.

"Ready to start your day?" asked Hoo-Lan cheerfully.

"I don't think so," I groaned.

"Tish-tush. We have too much to do for you to lie abed like this. Spit-spot, clip-clop, now's the time for all good men to come to the aid of their planet."

My grogginess vanished instantly. "Can you help me come to the aid of my planet?" I asked intently.

Hoo-Lan's big round nose twitched. "A figure of speech. I'm here to come to the aid of your brain. I'm your teacher, remember?"

I looked at him curiously. He stared back at me with huge, round eyes that almost dared me to read his mind. But of course I couldn't.

At least, not yet.

"First lesson," said Hoo-Lan, after I had found a bathroom and thrown some cold water on my face. "The uses of the URAT. You have already discovered some of them. I expect you would find many more on your own. But let's speed up the process."

"Fine with me," I said, settling into my wonderful chair.

"Right, then," said Hoo-Lan. "Now to begin with, the URAT is linked by microwave to the ship's main library. This means that it can find any kind of information almost instantly."

As it turned out, this also meant that the URAT could pull up fun stuff—plays and dances and concerts—from other worlds. If I wanted to go to the trouble, I could even hook it up to a holographic projector, which was truly amazing. Imagine being able to see a three-dimensional movie acted out in the middle of your living room—even a special effects extravaganza, with monsters, rocket battles, and alien landscapes. That's what this thing could do.

Next Hoo-Lan took me to the library itself, where they had machines you could actually plug yourself into so that you *experienced* stuff. These machines fooled all your senses; you didn't just see things—you tasted, touched, smelled, and heard them.

This was great for stories—though some of those alien stories were pretty weird, I want to tell you.

But it was even better for research.

Imagine your teacher has assigned a report on

Columbus's first voyage. With one of these machines, you would feel like you were right on one of his ships; you would feel the sea breezes, smell the sailors' body odor, taste the kind of food they ate.

If you're a browser like me—the kind of person who starts out looking up horses and winds up reading about ancient Greece—doing research this way is incredible.

For example: say that while you're studying Columbus, you get interested in a bird you see flying by your ship. Whisper a command, and the bird is in your hands! It's like a three-dimensional illustration you can pick up and feel. And while you examine it, the machine pours information about it into your head.

Now let's say you wonder how the bird sees the world. Say the word and you're inside its skin and *you're flying!*

As you fly, you spot an island that looks interesting. Dropping down for a landing, you leave the bird's body behind, and begin to walk along the beach.

It's hot, so you decide to go for a swim. You *feel* the water—and taste it, too. And all the while you're really just in a room, plugged into one of these machines.

Let me tell you, a guy can get lost inside these things!

In fact, I guess that's sort of a problem. From

what Hoo-Lan told me, when the machines were first invented, some beings got so fascinated by them that they never wanted to come out; a few got so involved in the machines they actually starved to death. So the ship's head librarian (who was purple and had twelve tentacles) had very strict rules about how long you could use the machines. She didn't want beings to get hooked.

Of course, I didn't learn all this stuff all at once. By the time Hoo-Lan was done showing me how to use the URAT that first day, I was pretty tired. I was also exhilarated, since the possibilities were so astonishing.

I was also depressed, because the more I saw of the alien technology, the more clear it became that Earth didn't stand a chance if they decided to do us in.

I felt like the future of the planet was in my hands, which at the moment seemed awfully small and weak.

As it turned out, I was wrong. Earth's destiny wasn't so much in my hands. It was in my brain.

However, since I considered my brain my most precious possession, I wasn't entirely happy when the aliens asked if they could have it.

CHAPTER THIRTEEN

Aliens Want My Brain

Actually, I suppose it would be more accurate to say that the aliens wanted to borrow my brain for a bit. I found out about it a couple of days after I had come on board the *New Jersey*. I had just climbed out of my hammock, and was getting ready to go order something to eat, when my URAT began to buzz.

Flipping it open, I saw Hoo-Lan. He looked upset. "Krepta, I need to speak to you. May I come to your room?"

"Could it wait until after I have something to eat?" I asked.

"Why don't I meet you in the dining area?" he replied.

That was fine with me. So we decided which dining area we would meet at—there were several thousand of them on board the ship. I punched the code into the transcendental elevator and stepped through the wall.

Hoo-Lan arrived in a pair of brilliant red shorts covered with tropical flowers and purple butterflies. We took a seat in a quiet corner.

"So what's up?" I asked.

Before he could answer, the alarm sounded, and we had to lie down on the floor while the ship made a leap across space.

"I wish they wouldn't always do that when I'm getting ready to eat," I groaned, when I was sitting at the table again.

"Someone did a study," replied Hoo-Lan. "It showed that, for no apparent reason, most jumps are made when the greatest number of beings are sitting down to eat." He punched a few buttons on the table, then looked up and added, "Sometimes the universe is just like that. By the way, did anyone tell you about the time component of the jumps?"

"Beg your pardon?" I asked, massaging my stomach and wondering if I would be able to eat or not.

"I take it that means 'No,' " said Hoo-Lan. A plate floated up from the center of the table. In the center was a pile of something that looked like marinated eyeballs.

I decided to skip breakfast. "Yes, it means no. Tell me about the time aspect."

"It's pretty simple, really. One thing that happens when we make one of those leaps across space is that while it takes only a minute of *our* time, the time passage in the outside world is quite a bit longer."

I wrinkled my brow. "I know that the faster we go, the slower time goes for us," I said.

I had learned that from all my science fiction reading. I knew that if we approached the speed of light, time inside the ship would come to a virtual standstill. This meant that if we spent a century traveling at the speed of light, those of us inside the ship would age by only a tiny fraction of that amount of time. But I had a feeling Hoo-Lan was saying something different.

"We're really not quite sure how it works," he confessed, when I asked him about it. "We just know that we start a space leap at one point, come out at another a few seconds later, and in the so-called real world, a whole lot of time has gone by."

"Wait a minute," I said. "How much time has gone by since I came on board?"

Hoo-Lan popped one of the eyeball-looking things into his mouth and bit down on it. The squishy sound made me wish we had decided to meet in my room instead.

"Can't say for sure," he said. "I don't always pay attention to that sort of thing. The ship travels at about half the speed of light most of the time. Between that and the space leaps we've taken, I'd guess that a month to a month and a half have gone by back on Earth."

I sat back in my chair, feeling slightly boggled. I had left on the 24th of May. From my point of view, about three days had gone by. But Susan Simmons might have done six weeks of living since then. It was weird: I was three days older and Susan was six weeks older. I wondered what it would feel like to go home and find that she was a grown up and I was still a kid.

I didn't care for the idea all that much.

I decided to change the subject. "What did you want to talk to me about?" I asked, looking at Hoo-Lan's plate and wondering if I wanted to try one of the things he was eating. I figured they couldn't possibly taste as bad as they looked.

Hoo-Lan poked at one of the things on his plate and a drop of green ooze came out.

I decided I didn't want to try them after all.

"I have been asked to get your reaction to an idea proposed by one of the members of the council that you broke in on the other day."

At first I was surprised that Hoo-Lan had heard about that incident. But if they had appointed him to be my tutor, I guess it made sense that they would keep him posted on what I was up to.

"What's the request?" I asked.

Hoo-Lan looked terribly uncomfortable. "You know the Interplanetary Council is engaged in a bitter struggle regarding what we are going to do about your planet. They would like your permission to tap your mind for some additional information."

"What do you mean, 'tap my mind'?"

Hoo-Lan ordered the table to take away the rest of his food. "First, they'll want to ask you a lot of questions. Then they'll probably hypnotize you, so that you can tell us things about your past that you have forgotten." He paused, then said, "Last of all, they'd like to do some brain work."

"Brain work?" I asked nervously.

"They're hoping if they dig around in there a bit, they may be able to find out what's wrong with you."

"What do you mean?" I yelped. "There's nothing wrong with me!"

Of course, that wasn't entirely true. I knew I was far from perfect. But I didn't think I needed brain surgery to fix my minor defects—or even my major ones.

"I don't mean you personally. I mean you earthlings. We're wondering if the problem is organic."

"What problem?" I asked, knowing full well what he was talking about.

"The general human problem," said Hoo-Lan patiently. "Your race's willingness to destroy your home, kill each other, let people starve—all that stuff."

All that stuff indeed! Did they think they would find the reasons for all that in *my* brain?

Suddenly a horrible thought struck me: what if the reasons *were* in my brain?

I don't mean just my brain. I mean every human brain. What if the problem is that there's something wrong with the way we're wired? Would that mean the mess we've made of things isn't our fault? And if so, would that mean things were hopeless, that we could never fix the mess?

Or could the aliens do something about it? What if by looking inside my head, they could find a way to help us change? What if by examining my brain, they could learn how to help us stop wars forever?

Maybe it was no big deal. After all, CrocDoc had already done a little work on my head, and I had been able to get up and walk away from the table as if nothing had happened.

"Just how much digging do they want to do?" I asked.

"We're talking a total cut and paste job," said Hoo-Lan. "Most of the work would be done with light and magnets and atomic probes, of course. And our doctors are pretty good. But still, there's no guarantee."

I swallowed hard. "No guarantee of what?"

Hoo-Lan looked straight into my eyes. "No guarantee that you'll ever be able to think again," he whispered.

CHAPTER FOURTEEN

Dissected!

I stared at Hoo-Lan. A few minutes ago I was having a hard time trying to decide what to have for breakfast. Now I was supposed to decide if I was willing to risk my brain for the sake of the planet I had abandoned.

I sat without speaking for a long time. I thought about home and school. I wasn't particularly eager to become a drooling moron for the sake of Duncan Dougal. But then I thought about the things I had seen on the news—kids in the Middle East getting blown up, potbellied babies starving in Africa, street kids in South America being killed just to get them out of the way.

"You don't have to answer right away," said Hoo-Lan. "And we won't force you. You are one of us now."

"Am I really?" I whispered.

It was true that I was one of them in that they had accepted me, taken me in. But had I really let go of Earth? Or did I have my heart in the stars—and my feet in Kennituck Falls?

Hoo-Lan said nothing.

I stared at the table, then turned away from him. There was so much yet to see, to do, to explore. I had found my way to the stars. I was the one—the kid from Earth who had made it out into the galaxy. And now I was being asked to risk it all for the crazies I had left behind.

I rubbed the spot on my arm where Duncan used to punch me when he had had a bad night at home.

I thought of those kids in Africa.

"When do we start?" I whispered.

Broxholm came to see me later that day. "You don't have to do this, you know," he said.

"Do you think I shouldn't?" I asked.

He tugged on his nose. "I'm just worried about you," he said.

"I'm worried, too," I replied. "But hey, one reason I left Earth was that I figured no one would miss me. So what difference does it make?"

Broxholm looked at me for a moment. "I believe you overheard that we have a communications problem. My early departure from Earth left our other agent in Kennituck Falls without some essential equipment. So I cannot prove anything to you. But I believe that if I could show you the people back there, you would find some that miss you very much. Susan Simmons, for example."

I didn't say anything. I didn't like to talk about how I felt about Susan.

Our conversation was interrupted when Hoo-Lan stepped through the wall. He was wearing green shorts covered with hummingbirds.

"They're ready for you, Krepta," he said.

I touched foreheads with Broxholm, which is his planet's way of saying farewell with honor, and followed Hoo-Lan through the transcendental elevator to the operating room.

CrocDoc was waiting for us.

"Pleased to see you again, Krepta," he said soberly. His red jaws were drawn back in something that looked like a grin, but wasn't.

I nodded to him, and he made a gesture which translated into, "I salute your sinus cavities"—something I'm sure had more meaning for him than it did for me.

Having brain surgery on the *New Jersey* is not the same as having it on Earth. I wasn't scrubbed and put into a hospital gown. I almost wish I had been; some kind of ritual might have made me feel better, or helped me take it more seriously. Maybe it was just my fear that made me feel disconnected, as if I were moving through a dream of some kind.

Anyway, CrocDoc had me lay down on a table, told me the operation was being monitored by several dozen other doctors from a wealth of worlds, and then pricked me in the ear with something that immediately knocked me unconscious.

For a while, the sense of being in a dream

increased. I felt like I was surrounded by mists, and trying to swim in molasses.

Voices seemed to whisper around me. Faces floated into my consciousness, some familiar, some totally unknown to me. Sometimes the familiar and the unfamiliar merged, or a face I had known all my life would stretch and pull into a strange new shape.

I saw Susan, Duncan, and Ms. Schwartz, and most of the other kids from school. If I could have thought about it, which I couldn't, I might have wondered if CrocDoc was touching nerves in my brain that were setting off specific memories—somehow tickling the areas where those images were stored.

I saw my father. He was crying.

I saw Duncan again. He was frightened. I tried to cry out, because I was sure that something had happened to him. Only I couldn't, of course, since I was sound asleep, with the top of my head off.

Then I saw a man, a tall man wearing a suit. He was sitting at a desk in what looked like a typical classroom. It was dark, as if he had been working late and never bothered to turn on the lights.

As far as I could tell, I had never seen him before.

In my vision, the man's face began to twist with emotion; I couldn't tell what emotion it was—it could have been fear, or anger, or sorrow, maybe some odd combination of all three. It was so intense, it was hard to label. But whatever it was, it slowly twisted his face until suddenly he shoved the desk forward so violently that it fell over, scattering the stuff on top all across the floor.

Standing, he strode across the room until he was facing the television set that sat on the far counter. His features still twisted with that unnameable emotion, he reached up and began to peel off his face.

The skin beneath the mask was blue. As he slowly pulled it upward, he revealed a huge white mustache, a comic nose, enormous eyes.

It was Hoo-Lan!

Trembling now, he raised his hand. The skin of the hand looked human, as if he was wearing a mask over that, too. But it began to glow, gently at first, then brighter and more intensely. As a howl that sounded like some unholy combination of pain and anger tore out of Hoo-Lan, a bolt of power surged from his fingertips and blasted the television set to pieces.

Then everything went black.

I wondered if I was dead.

CHAPTER FIFTEEN

Brains in a Bottle

When I woke up, Hoo-Lan was staring at me anxiously.

"How did you do that?" he asked.

"Do what?" I asked, still feeling groggy.

"*You were inside my head.* I could feel it. I want to know how you did it."

I blinked. "I didn't even know I *did* did it," I mumbled, too confused to remember the dream I had had while I was unconscious.

I did notice that my words were slurred and slow. Was I all right? I couldn't tell.

"Peter, talk to me!" said Hoo-Lan urgently.

"Let the boy be," ordered CrocDoc. "He's been through a lot."

"Am I—did you—how did it go?" I asked, finally getting the words right.

"It's hard to say," replied CrocDoc, looking at me with his huge eyes. "We have to run an intense analysis on the data I uncovered. I did manage to get this," he said proudly, holding up a clear container.

Inside the container was a brain.

"My brain!" I screamed. "You took out my brain!"

I tried to grab for my head, but my hands were tied down.

"Well yes, but just for a while," said CrocDoc. "I'm going to put it back when I'm done."

I had tried to jump off the table when I first saw the bottle with my brain in it. That failed completely—either because I was tied down, or simply had no control over my muscles at the moment. Just as well, since it wouldn't have been a good idea for me to go running around without any brains. (Although I knew a lot of people back on Earth who did it all the time.)

I took a deep breath, trying to calm down. I took a lot of deep breaths before it did any good.

"How come I can see?" I whispered, when I thought I had some control over myself.

"Oh, your brain is still hooked into your head," said CrocDoc. Holding up the bottle again, he gestured to the bottom of it. "See all these wires? They run into your skull, providing nerve attachments. I'll unplug them whenever we're going to do some work that might be uncomfortable for you. But in the meantime, you can finally join us here in the world of the waking."

"Finally?" I murmured. "How long have I been unconscious?"

"About ten days, Earth time," said Hoo-Lan.

93

"More than a week!" I cried. "They haven't done anything to Earth yet, have they?"

"No, no. All action is postponed pending analysis of your brain."

Typical of my life. In most of the stories I've read, the fate of the world is in the hero's hands. In my case, the fate of the world was somewhere in my brains—maybe in my temporal lobes, or my corpus callosum, or my medulla oblongata. Wherever they finally found what they were looking for. Or didn't find it, since there was no guarantee that the answer *was* in my brain. Just a possibility.

A buzzer sounded from the ceiling. CrocDoc pushed a button. "What is it?" he asked.

"May we come in?"

I thought I recognized the voice, but I couldn't be certain, since I was still feeling kind of groggy. Would I ever feel alert again? Or was I doomed to a life of permanent mental fuzz?

The worst thing was, in my current condition, I didn't really care. I couldn't even *make* myself care. I wondered vaguely if this was what it was like to be hooked on drugs.

"Do you feel like having visitors?" asked CrocDoc.

"Why not?" I said, though to tell you the truth, I really didn't care all that much at this point.

At once, Fleef and Gurk stepped through the wall.

"Oh, my," said Fleef, when she saw me strapped to the table, with my brain sitting on the counter next to me. Her face turned a deeper shade of orange, and the sphere on the stalk on her skull went "Neep! Neep!"

"How are you, Krepta?" asked Gurk. His big eyes seemed filled with worry.

"Okay, sort of," I said.

"We've been worried about you," said Fleef. "Everyone is very impressed with how brave you are."

"Does that mean you don't want to blow up Earth anymore?" I whispered.

"It means I hope we don't have to," replied Fleef, squeezing my hand.

I was disappointed. On the other hand, I suppose my being a good guy about all this didn't really reduce the possible menace of my planet. I sighed.

"We brought you something," said Gurk, trying to sound cheerful. He held up a bag. "Do you want to see?"

I tried to nod, but couldn't, because my head was strapped down. "Sure," I said. "Let's see."

He reached into the bag and pulled out a blob of fur.

"What is it?" I asked.

"It's a skimml," said Fleef. She sounded very pleased.

Gurk held the thing in front of my face. It was

about six inches across, round and red—which made it look something like a big furry ladybug. After a moment two stalks rose out of the fur. The eyes on the end of them looked at me and blinked.

"They're squishy." said Gurk. "And almost indestructible. See?"

With that, he squeezed the skimml's middle, which caused it to bulge out of the top and bottom of his hand.

"Lots of fur, no bones," said Fleef.

Gurk set the skimml on my stomach. It walked up and took another look at my face, walked back to my stomach, turned around three times, and settled down with a sigh. After a moment it began to make a noise something like a window fan.

"It likes you!" cried Fleef happily.

I named the skimml Murgatroyd. It kept me company through the following days as CrocDoc turned my brain on and off while he examined it. I had a lot of visitors. They all seemed to like to squeeze the skimml.

Broxholm showed up almost every day, as did Fleef and Gurk. Aliens I had never seen before stopped in to say hello. The crystal captain sent me a plant whose blossoms made singing noises that reminded me of my interview in the diamond chamber. And Hoo-Lan spent hours with me every day, telling me wonderful stories about the history of the galaxy.

Every once in a while he would look at me strangely, and ask me questions about what had happened to me while I was having the operation. But CrocDoc was always there, and wouldn't let him question me too sharply.

Finally the day came when CrocDoc was going to put my brain back in my head.

"Did you find what you needed?" I asked, still feeling groggy and disconnected.

His snout drooped down. "Not yet," he said. "But we're still analyzing the data. Don't despair, Krepta. All is not lost."

And then he put me to sleep.

When I woke up, the skimml was whirring on my stomach, and my brain was back in my head. CrocDoc was leaning over me, just as he had that first day, after he had put in the language implant.

"Am I all right?" I whispered.

"With any luck, you'll be better than ever," he said.

I opened and closed my eyes a few times, and looked around the room. My vision was sharp and clear. I stretched, and realized that my hands were no longer tied down.

"Can I stand up?" I asked.

"No reason not to," said CrocDoc. "Just take it easy."

"Why don't you come up here?" I said, lifting Murgatroyd from my stomach to my shoulder. Murgatroyd snuggled in as I sat up and swung my legs over the edge of the table.

"Careful," said CrocDoc.

I waited a moment before standing up. But I felt terrific. It was as if my brain had been wrapped in fog, and now the fog was gone.

CrocDoc made a gesture that meant "I put my hand beneath your grandmother's egg," and told me how much he appreciated my help. "You may come and talk to me any time about our findings," he said. "I owe you that courtesy at least."

I gathered my things, the little gifts that aliens had brought me, squeezed Murgatroyd for luck, and prepared to return to my room.

But when I stepped through the transcendental elevator, it spit me out into a place I had never seen before.

CHAPTER SIXTEEN

Duncan

I was in a chamber filled with machinery. I recognized some of the devices as things the aliens used for communicating across space.

To my right was a kind of desk. Sitting on the desk was a helmet.

"Put it on," said a voice behind me.

I jumped in surprise, which caused Murgatroyd to squeak in protest. "Hoo-Lan," I snapped, spinning to face him. "Don't do things like that to me."

"Sorry," said the little alien. "I keep forgetting how skittish you are."

"I assume you're the one who brought me here."

Hoo-Lan reached out for the skimml. I handed it to him. "You assume correctly," he said, kneading the red ball of fur between his hands until Murgatroyd began to thrum with contentment.

"Would you mind telling me why?"

"Put on the helmet," replied Hoo-Lan.

I looked at the helmet nervously. "Is it safe?" I asked. As soon as the words were out of my mouth I thought, *Well, that was a stupid question, Peter. He won't tell me if it's not, so why bother to ask!*

But Hoo-Lan spread his hands and said, "No, not entirely,"—which just goes to show how much I knew.

"Then why do you want me to put it on? Haven't I taken enough risks already?"

"I ask because the possible benefit outweighs the risk," said Hoo-Lan. "Put it on."

I hesitated, then sat down at the table and put on the helmet. At Hoo-Lan's direction, I moved a couple of the control balls on the table in front of me.

And then I was inside Duncan Dougal's head. I shouted so loud that the skimml squawked and jumped out of Hoo-Lan's hands. It lay flat on the floor, stretched out and shivering, its eye stalks shooting up and down as it looked for trouble.

"For heaven's sakes, be quiet!" hissed Hoo-Lan, bending down to pick up Murgatroyd.

At least, I think that's what he said. I was too enmeshed in what was happening inside my head to pay attention to him.

I'm not sure how I knew that I was inside Duncan's head so quickly. It's not like there were any labels saying: THIS IS DUNCAN DOUGAL'S BRAIN.

Maybe I knew just because it *was* Duncan's

brain, and his identity was stamped on every cell and synapse.

I felt uncomfortable about this. Little as I liked Duncan, I didn't think I had any right to poke around inside his brain. *Duncan*, I thought. *Duncan, can you hear me?*

No answer; either he wasn't aware of me, or wasn't able to answer, or was answering and it wasn't coming through.

Things happen fast inside a human brain. I started looking around. In a matter of seconds—or less, maybe; I don't know exactly how long it took—I had learned more about Duncan Dougal's life than I ever wanted to know.

Speaking from my point of view, here are some of the most important things I learned:

1) Part of the reason Duncan was such a beast was the way he got whacked around at home.

2) He was incredibly intelligent (this totally astonished me, until I found out more about it).

3) He was a sadder person than I ever would have guessed and

4) He had talked with my father not long ago, and my father was terribly upset about my leaving. Believe me, that last one was a shock to me.

Duncan, I thought again, *can you hear me?*

Still no answer. I took one last, quick look around the inside of his head, then raised the helmet from my own head.

Hoo-Lan was looking at me eagerly.

"What is going on here?" I hissed.

"You mean you got through?" he whispered. His voice sounded almost hungry.

"What is going on?" I asked again, tired of giving more answers than I got.

But Hoo-Lan wasn't ready to explain yet. Instead, he looked at me for a long moment, then answered my question with another question. Namely, "How would you like to visit another planet?"

I knew he was changing the subject, but I couldn't help myself. "When can we go?" I asked eagerly.

"How about now?" Passing Murgatroyd back to me, he led me to a circle printed on the floor. "Stand here," he ordered. "And as you value your life—don't move!"

He crossed the room and fiddled with some dials, then crossed back and positioned himself next to me. Almost instantly a blue beam shone down from the ceiling, and the room faded from sight.

When I opened my eyes, I was on a tiny bit of sand in the middle of a huge body of water.

It was night, and the sky above us was unlike anything I had ever seen—a vast sheet of black filled with stars. All right, that's not so weird. But their patterns were unfamiliar, and their light was so bright you could read by it. In the sky to our right floated a small green moon. A ribbon of shimmering, changing color stretched from horizon to horizon.

"All right!" I shrieked.

"Shhh!" said Hoo-Lan. "There are some very big animals around here. We don't want to attract their attention if we can avoid it."

I squeezed Murgatroyd and looked around nervously. I couldn't see any big animals. But who knew what form they might take here? For all I knew, the island we were standing on was actually some enormous sea creature. I looked down, half expecting to see a huge mouth in the sand.

"How did we get here?" I whispered.

"We took a ship-to-surface elevator," said Hoo-Lan. "It's like moving around inside the ship, but on a grander scale."

"Why didn't Broxholm use one of these when he came to Earth?" I asked, remembering our trip from Kennituck Falls to the *New Jersey*.

"Because first you have to set them up," said Hoo-Lan.

"Why would anybody set one up out here in the middle of nowhere?"

"*I* set it up, to be a private place. I like to come here to think."

I glanced at Hoo-Lan, who was easy to see because he was glowing again. "Who are you?" I asked.

"Your teacher," he said, as if that answered

everything. "And as your teacher, I want you to see some things here."

He pulled a thin tube out of one of his pockets and blew a little tune on it. A moment later I heard the tune repeated somewhere across the water, as if it were being sung by a bird—or, for all I knew, some strange kind of fish. Or something else altogether, for that matter.

I turned to Hoo-Lan. He put his fingers to his lips and motioned me to silence.

We waited. The tune was repeated again, off in another direction, and then again, and again. Suddenly I saw a commotion in the water, as something bright and huge rose from the depths to the edge of the island.

"Our chariot arrives," said Hoo-Lan.

My eyes were fixated on the green thing waiting just beneath the surface of the water. It was at least a hundred feet long. If it was a chariot, it was a strange one, because it was clearly a living animal—either that, or a very good imitation of one.

Hoo-Lan played another little tune. The creature rose to the surface and tipped back its head, which was the size of a small room. Its huge silver tongue extended to the shore like a gangplank.

"Go ahead," said Hoo-Lan. "Step aboard!"

CHAPTER SEVENTEEN

Rhoomba Ride, Hoo-Lan's Home

Have you ever walked on a tongue? It's an odd feeling. The surface is firm but squishy, and it's a little hard to keep your balance.

I glanced behind me, to make sure Hoo-Lan was coming. Not that I didn't trust him. But walking into a mouth is pretty scary.

He nodded to me.

Clutching Murgatroyd, I walked on.

Hoo-Lan caught up with me as I reached the creature's teeth. They were taller than me, and made me think of huge icicles. Once we were clear of its fangs, the beast drew in its tongue, pulling us so far into its mouth that I was afraid we were going to be swallowed after all. Then it closed its mouth, and for a moment we *were* swallowed—by darkness.

That ended when Hoo-Lan began to glow. The blue light reflecting off the beast's silvery tongue made everything look strange and ghostly.

"Where are we going?" I whispered. Not that I thought the beast would hear us. It was just one of those places that made you want to whisper.

"We're going to my home," Hoo-Lan replied. He looked happy.

"Are we going across the water—or under it?"

"Oh, under. Definitely under. Rhoombas don't like to go on top of the water if they can help it."

"Rhoombas?"

"That's what you're riding in now," said Hoo-Lan. "They're one of the best ways to get around on this world."

"Do they ever, well—you know, do they have *accidents*?" I asked. I couldn't quite bring myself to come right out and ask if they ever made a mistake and swallowed their passengers.

"No one's perfect," said Hoo-Lan with a shrug. I realized he was speaking in English again.

"Why are you doing that?"

"What did you see inside my head?"

I looked at him for a moment. "What do you mean?"

"I mean if you tell me what you saw, I'll tell you why I'm speaking English."

I hesitated, for two reasons. First, I wasn't sure just what I *had* seen when I was in Hoo-Lan's head; I needed a moment to think about it. Second, any time someone wants to know something *that* badly it makes me a little nervous.

"I've spent a lot of time studying the Earth," said Hoo-Lan, still in English. "Fascinating place."

Something Broxholm had said when I first came onto the spaceship floated to the top of my memory. "Hoo-Lan, did you name the *New Jersey*?"

"You get a cigar for that one," he said, putting his finger beside his nose.

"*Who are you?*" I asked, for the third time since I had known him.

"All take and no give makes for a lopsided friendship. Tell me what you saw in my head."

I closed my eyes and thought for a moment. "You were in a classroom. Only you didn't look like yourself. You were in disguise—sort of the way Broxholm was, when he took over our class. It was night. You were angry about something, angry enough that you began to glow until it was so bright it showed right through your mask. So angry you blew up a TV set."

He stared at me with a look that was something like horror. "Have you told this to anyone else?"

I shook my head.

"Please don't."

"Did it really happen?" I asked.

Before he could answer, a low, groaning sound rumbled around us. "Ah, we've arrived," said Hoo-Lan. "We'll talk more about this later."

"Arrived where?"

"At the city under the sea."

"But how are we supposed to get out?" I cried.

I didn't mind getting wet, but I knew if we were deep enough, the water pressure would crush us.

"Step back here," answered Hoo-Lan, leading me further into the Rhoomba's throat. After we had gone about ten feet we came to a kind of chamber, a round area that went straight up.

Once Hoo-Lan was sure I was standing in the right place, he slapped the wall of the chamber three times. The Rhoomba roared and a mighty gust of wind sent us flying straight up, as if we were being shot through a whale's blowhole.

I landed on a padded surface, inside a small room. I was still trying to recover from the surprise when I saw a being who resembled Hoo-Lan drop something down the Rhoomba's blowhole, which was pressed against an opening in the floor. You could see the Rhoomba's leathery green flesh all around the edges.

"Reward," said the stranger, when he saw my questioning look. Then he drew a trapdoor shut across the opening, sealing off the little room.

No sooner was the trapdoor shut than a door in the side of the room opened and three more beings who were clearly of Hoo-Lan's race came running into the room. They wore light green togas, not brightly colored shorts. One by one, they clapped Hoo-Lan on the back, then gave him a big hug.

When they were done greeting Hoo-Lan, they turned to me and cried "Welcome, Krepta!"

"Thank you," I said, feeling a little shy.

Clutching Murgatroyd for comfort, I followed them out of the little room, still wishing Hoo-Lan had finished telling me why he was so wound up about what I had seen inside his head.

My questions faded when I passed through the door of the little room and found myself standing in the center of a great city of tree-lined streets, soaring buildings, and busy markets.

Something about the city struck me as odd. It took me a few minutes to figure out that the place had almost no sharp edges. The buildings, even the tallest ones, were smooth and rounded, and had a soft, almost gentle look. Some of them were covered with decorations. I don't know what they were made of, but the colors were mostly soft shades of blue and green and yellow, with here and there a deeper, stronger color that kept things interesting.

Even more striking than the buildings was the fact that the city was completely encased in a clear dome that stretched far above the top of the tallest building that I could see.

On the other side of the dome, above and all around the city, was water.

"Hoo-Lan," I whispered. "It's wonderful!"

"I'm glad you like it," he said, patting a six-

legged animal that happened to be walking by. "I'm very proud of it."

We spent the whole day touring the city. It was beyond anything I had ever imagined. The rhoomba that delivered us was typical of the way things worked here; much of what needed to be done was taken care of by animals that had been trained and bred to the task. My favorites were the trash munchers. Every home and store had one—a fat little beast that loved to eat all kinds of garbage.

"Cuts down on the mess," said the little blue woman who first explained them to me.

All the animals seemed happy and well cared for.

All the people did, too.

After a while I began to get suspicious. I knew enough about cities to feel like something was missing.

"Don't you have anyone hungry here, anyone without a home?" I asked at last.

"Why should we?"

"I don't think you *should*," I said. "I just didn't know there could be a city without people like that."

"There can't, on your planet. The difference is that we've made a decision that it's not going to be that way. There's enough to go around, you know. Enough here, and enough on Earth. It's not like people *have* to be cold and hungry. You just haven't decided it's a bad idea."

"Of course we think it's a bad idea!"

"No, you *think* you think it's a bad idea. If your people, all your people, really believed it was a bad idea, they would stop talking about it and change things so it didn't happen anymore."

I squeezed Murgatroyd, trying to keep from getting angry about what Hoo-Lan had said. I had a feeling he was blaming me, personally, for everything that was wrong on Earth.

We had this argument outside a huge building. "Come on," said Hoo-Lan. "There's something in here I want to show you."

People in the building greeted him as if he were an old friend. That was nothing surprising; it had been happening all day. One of the weirder things about the visit was the feeling I got that the whole city knew my teacher.

A series of long, snakelike creatures lifted us from floor to floor, until we were near the top of the building. On every floor, people shouted greetings to Hoo-Lan.

"Who are you?" I asked again, when we were standing outside a door on the top floor of the building.

Hoo-Lan smiled. "Why don't you look into my brain and find out?"

CHAPTER EIGHTEEN

Contact!

Hoo-Lan led me into a room filled with all sorts of fascinating equipment.

"You know," he said, as he began tinkering with some machinery, "I've spent a good part of my life trying to crack the secrets of telepathy."

"You mean direct communication from one mind to another?" I asked.

He nodded. "The thing is," he continued, staring at me intently, "*you've* got it. You went into my brain while you were being operated on and pulled out images. Jumbled ones, of course," he added hastily. "But you did pull them out of my head, and you did it without training. I think something that happened on the operating table helped unleash the ability in you."

He took the skimml from me and began squishing it back and forth. "You can't understand what this means, Krepta, unless you know that we've been trying for lifetimes to create this ability in some of our people. By *we*, I mean the Interplanetary League. The best we've been able to do so far is piggyback on thought transmission with some of our machines. That's the situation with your friend Duncan, by the way."

"He's not my friend!" .

I regretted the words the instant they were out of my mouth. They made me sound small and petty. "What do you mean, anyway?" I asked, trying to cover up my stupid remark.

"Well, one of the early problems we had with star travel was that radio messages only move at the speed of light. Of course, this made it almost impossible to communicate between places that were light-years apart. We finally managed to invent a hyper-space transmitter, which gave us nearly instant contact between stars. Unfortunately, Broxholm had the only one on your planet. So when he was forced to flee, our remaining agent in Kennituck Falls, a female named Kreeblim, was left without a way to communicate with the ship after it had moved out of your solar system.

"To get around this, she used a brain enhancer on Duncan."

"You mean she made him smart?" I cried. That explained what I had found when I connected with Duncan back on the mother ship.

"No, she didn't *make* him smart," said Hoo-Lan. "She simply unleashed some of his basic potential. You humans are so much smarter than you act, it's appalling. Anyway, since thought is instant, by sending her messages through his brain, she is once more able to communicate with us."

"So what's the big deal about telepathy? Sounds like you already have it."

Hoo-Lan shook his head. "No," he said, passing Murgatroyd back to me. "It's not the same as direct mind-to-mind communication. *That's* what I'm after. That's what *you* managed when you tapped into my head. And when you got through to Duncan Dougal today, before we left the ship, you managed it without the brain treatments and mechanical connections we have to use for such a communication. Only three beings on the *New Jersey* could have made that connection. And each of them has had extensive training and repeated brain stimulation, and has to be *in* a force field with hardware attached to do it."

He looked at me. "But you—you did it without even trying. The secret is in there," he said, pointing at my forehead, which he was too short to reach. "Just like the reason for Earth's violence."

I was sick of everyone thinking I had all the answers. "This isn't the *Encyclopaedia Britannica*, you know," I said, tapping my head myself. (Though I must admit I'd read quite a bit of the *EB*.) Then another thought struck me. "You don't want to do more brain surgery on me, do you?" I asked, taking a step backward.

Hoo-Lan took my hand. "I just want to see if

we can talk to each other," he said, leading me to a machine that looked like the one I had seen in the communication room on the ship.

"You stand here," said Hoo-Lan, positioning me under a metallic pyramid. "And I'll sit over here, where I can get some readings on what's going on inside your head. If you make contact, try using these dials to fine tune things. If things get too intense, punch this escape button."

The whole thing had happened so fast I didn't have time to think about whether or not I wanted to do it. I clutched Murgatroyd, feeling frightened and hopeful at the same time.

Hoo-Lan turned on the machine and said, "Now concentrate! Try to read my mind!"

I did as he asked. But instead of connecting with Hoo-Lan, I found myself back in contact with Duncan!

I couldn't believe it. Light-years away from Earth, visiting a distant planet, and who do I end up in a psychic link with? Duncan Dougal!

I mean, gimme a break, folks.

Duncan wasn't much happier than I was, though he didn't know I was there yet. Actually, he was feeling something that I had felt more than once since this all started: unhappiness that other worlds had been watching us as we bumbled along, blowing each other up and starving ourselves when there was enough food for everyone. *It's embarrassing*, he told himself.

It certainly is, I thought at him.

This time he heard me! I knew, because I was so linked to him that I could tell he wondered if he was losing his mind. *Who is that?* he thought.

Come on, Duncan—don't you know who I am?

Peter? he thought in astonishment. *Peter Thompson?*

None other! Wait, let me try something here. I fiddled with the dials Hoo-Lan had showed me.

Where are you? asked Duncan.

Shhh! Wait!

He was bursting with curiosity. But he waited while I tinkered with the machine, which was a little like adjusting the antenna on a television set. Suddenly I got complete focus: not only was I inside Duncan's brain, but Duncan was inside *my* brain.

To tell you the truth, I wasn't sure I liked the idea. I mean, in the past about the only way Duncan had communicated with me was through noogies and black eyes. But here we were, worlds apart, linked solely by our minds. So it was pretty exciting, even if it *was* Duncan. I could hear his thoughts as clearly as if he were speaking to me, instead of merely thinking.

"Where are you?" he asked.

"In space, silly. Where did you expect I would be? Oh, Duncan, it's glorious. The stars! I can't tell you. But it's frightening, too. There's a lot going on. Big things. And Earth is right in the middle of it. *We're* right in the middle of it."

"What do you mean?"

"The Interplanetary Council—that's sort of a galaxywide United Nations—is trying to figure out what to do about us. We've got their tails in a tizzy because our planet is so weird. From what Broxholm has told me—"

"Wait!" he replied. "Tell me about Broxholm. Is he treating you all right?"

"Well, that's kind of weird, too," I said. "I'm never quite sure what's going on with him. But listen, I've got to tell you this stuff first, because I'm not sure how long I can stay on, and you have to get word out to someone. Here's the deal. The aliens are having a big debate among themselves about how to handle the Earth. And I don't mean just Broxholm's gang. We're talking about hundreds of different planets here. As near as I can make out, they've narrowed it down to four basic approaches. One group wants to take over Earth, one group wants to leave us on our own, one group wants to blow the planet to smithereens, and one group wants to set up a blockade."

"*What?*"

"They say it's for the sake of the rest of the galaxy. They seem to find us pretty scary, Duncan."

"I don't get it."

"Don't ask me to explain how an alien's mind

works," I snapped. "As far as I can make out, they think there's something wrong with us. Well, two things, actually. The first is the way we handle things down there. That's why they've been sending in people like Broxholm; they're supposed to study us and figure out why we act the way we do.

"So Broxholm was some kind of anthropologist—?"

"You could put it that way," I replied. I was astonished Duncan knew the word, until I remembered what had happened to him. "Anyway, the other thing that has them concerned is how smart we could be if we ever got our act together. Broxholm actually seems jealous. Every once in a while he goes on about the human brain being the most underused tool in the galaxy. I get the impression they're afraid if we learn to use our full intelligence before we get civilized—"

"We're civilized!" cried Duncan in indignation.

"Not by their standards. Anyway, they're afraid—"

I didn't finish the sentence. Someone had entered the chamber. I heard a lot of scuffling and squawking.

"Uh-oh," I said. "Something's happening. I gotta go, Duncan."

I pushed the escape button. Only I wished I hadn't, because the sight that greeted me when I came out of my trance nearly broke my heart.

CHAPTER NINETEEN

The Fading Glow

Hoo-Lan lay on the floor, stretched out straight and stiff as a board. Several of the little blue people were gathered around him, squawking in dismay.

"What is it?" I cried, rushing over to him. "What's happened?"

"The leader!" cried a green-haired woman. "What have you done to the leader?"

"It was the machine!" cried one of the men. "He knew he shouldn't use the machine!"

"No, it's not the machine," another one shouted. "It's him. It's the earthling!"

"What do you mean?" I asked. "What's wrong with Hoo-Lan?"

Before anyone could answer, the room was filled with a loud buzzing sound. It took me a moment to realize that the noise was coming from both Hoo-Lan's URAT and mine.

"The ship!" cried one of the men. "The ship is leaving. You must get him back to the ship!"

"But he's sick!" I said, nearly sick with fear myself.

"Yes. But he must be on the ship. Besides, his doctor is there. You must go back to the ship."

Gathering around Hoo-Lan's stiff body, the blue men and women picked him up and carried him to the room next door. The buzzing of the URAT grew more urgent.

"Stand here!" said one of the women, motioning to a circle on the floor. "Stand here!"

They put Hoo-Lan next to me. The men were pulling on their mustaches—a sign, my translator told me, of extreme grief.

"But what happened to him—?"

My words were cut off as a beam of blue light shot down from the ceiling, and we were sucked out of the city beneath the sea, through space, and back into the *New Jersey*.

I blinked. We were back in the room where we had started. "Hoo-Lan!" I cried, kneeling beside him. "Hoo-Lan, talk to me!"

He said nothing, only groaned a little. He was glowing, but only faintly.

Suddenly the alarm sounded. The ship was about to make a jump. I threw myself on the floor beside Hoo-Lan. Clutching Murgatroyd, who was chittering in alarm, I braced myself for the jump—and hoped that Hoo-Lan would live through it.

The horrible, high-pitched whine tore through the room, drowning my own moans of nausea. The tearing feelings began, became unbearable, and then ended. I lay next to Hoo-Lan, trembling and trying to recover, wondering how many light-years we had jumped, where we were now.

When I could push myself to my knees, I stared at Hoo-Lan. His glow was even fainter than before. I knew that he was dying.

I grabbed my URAT. "Give me the code for CrocDoc!" I cried. The moment the colored dots began to flash on the screen I raced across the room and punched the destination into the elevator. Then I ran back and tried to pick up Hoo-Lan. He was heavier than I thought, and his body was rigid, but I finally managed to get him into my arms.

Worried that I wouldn't get back across the room before the elevator did an automatic shut-off, I struggled toward the wall. The shut-off alarm sounded just as I pitched forward, falling through the wall and into CrocDoc's office.

Only CrocDoc wasn't there.

"Find him!" I shouted at the URAT. "Find CrocDoc."

The machine gave me another code. Leaving Hoo-Lan on the floor, I hurtled through the wall. Interrupting a meeting of some sort, I grabbed CrocDoc by the arm and said, "Your office! Quickly!"

To my relief, he didn't try to brush me off; instead, he immediately followed me back through the wall to his office.

I slumped against the wall in relief. I had done what I could do. Or so I thought. CrocDoc asked me to help him get Hoo-Lan onto the table. He was examining him while I watched in fascinated horror when Broxholm's voice came from the ceiling.

"Peter, you are wanted in the Council Room. The elevator is programmed. Please step through the wall."

"But Broxholm—"

"Come at once!"

"Better go," said CrocDoc. "I'll take care of things here."

"But is he—will he—?"

"I make no guarantees," said CrocDoc. "However I believe he will still be here when you get back."

Be here? What did that mean? Still on the table, but dead as a tubeless television? I started to say something, but Broxholm's voice thundered through the speaker.

"Now, Peter!"

"Best go," whispered CrocDoc.

I went.

Broxholm was waiting for me when I entered the chamber. So was the rest of the alien council, the eight beings I had encountered the first time I entered this room.

"Peter Thompson—Krepta—Child of the Stars—" said the sea-green alien. "The time is fast approaching when we will make a decision regarding the fate of the Earth."

I considered bolting right then, racing off to the communication room to see if I could get one last message off to Duncan, somehow get him to warn the government, someone, anyone, who might be able to do something. Then at least the Earth might have a fighting chance.

"We offer you a chance to speak in Earth's defense," said the alien who hung on the rack. "Tell us something we do not know, something that might give us cause to think again as we deliberate."

"You need to ask someone else," I said desperately. "I'm only a kid! What can I tell you?"

"Then you refuse to speak on behalf of the planet?" asked the purple alien.

"No! That's not what I mean! I just don't know what to say. I haven't lived enough, seen enough. I know there must be more good things out there than I have seen, things worth saving, things too wonderful too lose. *I know it!*"

"Yet you chose to leave," said one of the aliens who had not spoken before this, a dark creature who looked more like a shadow than anything real and solid.

"I chose to leave, not to destroy it," I said.

"All leaving involves a kind of destruction," said the shadow. "The chick destroys the egg in hatching. No home is the same once someone has gone from it."

"Why don't you help us?" I cried. "You have answers, you can fix things."

"You don't need our answers," said another alien. "Your problem is not shortage of food, or land. You live on one of the most blessed planets in the galaxy—or at least you used to, until you fouled it so. What could we offer you but technology? And what would you do with it but create new problems? The technology is not the problem. Hearts and minds, those are the problem."

"Send me back," I said, hardly able to believe the words were coming out of my mouth. "Let me find a reason for you. I won't run away. I'm not afraid for myself. But I don't want you to hurt my friends. I don't want you to hurt my father!"

I stopped, astonished at what I had just said.

"Leave us for a time," said the sea-green alien. "We need to deliberate."

I looked at Broxholm. He nodded.

I left the chamber.

CHAPTER TWENTY

Hoo-Lan's Wish

I didn't even program the elevator, since I figured the aliens would send me wherever they wanted me to go. Somewhat to my surprise, I found myself back at CrocDoc's.

Hoo-Lan lay on the table, rigid and unmoving, his glow dimmer than ever.

"How is he?" I whispered.

"Not good," said CrocDoc.

I stood for a moment, staring at my friend, my teacher. "Can I do anything for him?" I asked quietly.

"No."

"I'll be back," I said.

Moving quietly across the room, I instructed the URAT to send me back to the communication chamber where I had first made contact with Duncan. Glancing over my shoulder, feeling guilty for leaving, even though there was nothing I could do, I stepped through the wall.

What had happened to Hoo-Lan when he tried to make mental contact with me? Was this my fault? Was my human brain so poisonous it had done something terrible to his mind?

Once I reached the communication chamber, it took me a while to make contact with Duncan again. I wondered if he was still in the force field. After all, even though it had been only a couple of hours by my time since I spoke to him, the ship had made a space-shift since then. How much time had passed on Earth?

I fiddled with the controls, until I made contact with Duncan Dougal, my old enemy, my new ally. As I began to fine-tune the connection, it occurred to me that if this Kreeblim character they had mentioned had put Duncan in the force field, it might not be a good idea for me to say too much until I knew whether or not she was there.

"Duncan," I thought. "Is there anybody there?"

"Just you and me."

"Good." I finished focusing the connection, so we could see each other. "Listen, things are heating up out here. The aliens are planning something. I don't know what, but it's big. You have to get word to the government."

Duncan was explaining why he thought that was a stupid idea when we heard someone coming up the attic stairs.

"Pretend I'm not here," I said desperately. "I can't be caught talking to you like this. I'll try to hold on, but I'll break the connection if I have to.

"I understand," said Duncan.

But the person who showed up at the top of the stairs was no menace. Well, aside from the fact that the sight of her did something strange to my insides.

It was Susan Simmons, and I suddenly realized I had missed her more than I had guessed. I sighed. Why couldn't the aliens have hooked me into *her* brain?

With the URAT to help me, I told Susan how to free Duncan from the force field. Once she had him out, I was a little surprised to find that Duncan and I were still in contact.

When he said that he was surprised as well, I replied, "Of course. Your head is what we call wetware—an organic machine. At the moment, you happen to be one of the most powerful communication devices in the galaxy, Duncan. Now listen, I've got some important stuff to tell you. There are big things happening up here, and you need to—oh no!"

The last words came out as a shout of terror, because a pair of hands had just grabbed me by the back.

"You shouldn't do things like that, Peter," said Broxholm, turning me around and picking me up so that I had to stare straight into his huge orange eyes. "It makes it harder for us to trust you."

I wondered how much Broxholm had heard of what I had just told Duncan and Susan. Then I realized he couldn't have heard any of it, since it had all been done inside my head!

"The Council wants to see you again," said Broxholm. Carrying me across the room, he stepped through the transcendental elevator and back into the council chamber.

"What do you know about the fall of Hoo-Lan?" asked the sea-green alien, as soon as I was standing before the council again. He seemed sterner than ever, maybe even angry.

I hesitated. "He tried to connect himself to my mind," I said. "It happened to him then."

The other members of the council stirred restlessly. I got the sense I had said or done something wrong.

"Hoo-Lan was a fool," said the alien with purple tentacles.

Something inside me snapped. I had had enough of their superiority, their all-powerful lording it over me. I liked Hoo-Lan. No, I loved Hoo-Lan. He had been kind and gentle to me, taught me things, cared for me.

"Don't you say that!" I cried, rushing toward the alien.

I suppose it wasn't the best demonstration of how earthlings might be expected to control themselves. It didn't make any difference; I ran right through him without touching him.

I stopped, turned around, blinked in dismay.

I walked back toward the alien, waving my arms. They passed back and forth through his purple body.

"Broxholm!" I cried. "What's going on!"

He looked startled. "Did you really think they were here?" he asked. Then he blinked and said, "Do you realize who these beings are?"

"The people in charge of the ship?" I asked uncertainly.

Broxholm's nose twitched. The images of the other eight aliens responded with their various forms of laughter.

"These are the chief leaders of the Interplanetary Council," said Broxholm.

I ran back to his side, stunned at what he was saying. I had just tried to punch out one of the rulers of the galaxy!

For a kid who considers himself an intellectual, this was not the high point of my emotional life.

"What are they doing here?" I whispered. "Or not doing here?" I added, trying to salvage some dignity with a little humor.

"We generally meet via holographic projection," said a red alien, who looked sort of like a pile of seaweed. "It is simplest that way, as it allows us to stay on our own planets, and yet remain in contact. That way, we can hold our meetings anywhere we wish."

"As to your defense of Hoo-Lan," said the purple alien I had tried to clobber, "the emotion is admirable even if your way of expressing it is deplorable—and totally typical of your kind."

For a moment I had a terrible feeling they were going to blow up the planet because I had lost my temper. That was more guilt than I wanted to deal with!

"However you misunderstand our relationship with your mentor. Hoo-Lan was once a *member* of this council. He chose to resign, to pursue other interests. We have the utmost respect for him. We merely think he is wrongheaded."

"He has sent us a message," said the shadow. "I fear it may be the last message we will ever have from him."

I felt a lump begin to form in my throat. Had being in touch with my brain killed him? Were the people of Earth *that* terrible?

"Ever so gloomy," said Red Seaweed to the shadow. "Hoo-Lan may yet rejoin us."

"May and may not," replied the shadow. "Nonetheless, while you know that I favor the destruction of the Earth, I am willing to hold back in favor of what may be Hoo-Lan's last request."

"What was his last request?" I asked, my voice trembling.

"That we perform one final study of the Earth before we make our decision," said the shadow. "Personally, I think this is an enormous waste of time. But out of respect for a fallen comrade, I accede to his wishes, which specifically call for you and Broxholm to return to Earth and, with the help of the agent who is already in place there, file a final report."

"Those in favor?" asked Sea-green.

The vote was unanimous.

CHAPTER TWENTY-ONE

Home to Home

Once these aliens made up their minds, they weren't ones to dillydally. Within minutes Broxholm and I were riding a blue beam from the ship to the Earth.

One reason we could do that was that the last space-shift had brought us back into Earth orbit. The transporter beam only had a range of a few hundred thousand miles.

I think that the funniest thing I ever saw in my life was the look on Duncan's face when Broxholm and I shimmered into place in Kreeblim's attic.

That was the funniest thing. The most beautiful thing (I can't believe I'm saying this!) was Susan Simmons's face.

Of course, part of what made it so lovely to me was how glad she was to see me.

"Peter!" she cried, running over and throwing her arms around me.

I was a little embarrassed. "Hi, Susan," I said. "It's nice to see you."

Gak! "Nice to see you." How stupid! That was

a tenth, a thousandth of what I *wanted* to say to her. Only I didn't know how—especially with everyone else around us.

Broxholm broke the awkwardness of the moment in his own stiff way. "Good evening, Miss Simmons, Mr. Dougal," he said, nodding his green head. "I can't say it is exactly a pleasure to see you again, but since we are going to be working together, I hope that we will be able to put the past behind us."

For Broxholm, it was a pretty gracious speech.

"Working together?" asked Susan.

"How would you like to save the Earth?" I asked, trying to sound casual and heroic.

We didn't give them much chance to answer, to tell you the truth. Within minutes I led the way back to the takeoff position. Duncan positioned himself between me and Susan, which was annoying. I told myself to ignore it; from tapping into his brain, I knew what he had been through in the last month.

Of course, I had been through a lot myself.

The blue beam shimmered around us. We were dissolved into electrons and hurtled into space, then reformed inside the great alien ship that I had ridden to the stars.

Somewhere below us was the planet we had to save.

Somewhere below us was my father.

Somewhere in the ship was a little blue alien

who had made a dying wish that the Earth would have a final chance.

We had to honor that, try with all our hearts to save the planet.

We had to honor him.

I hoped that somehow he would live, so that Susan and Duncan could meet him.

Seconds later Kreeblim and Broxholm arrived.

"You're lucky," I told Susan and Duncan. "Traveling by transport beam saves you a trip through the disinfecting process."

"Disinfecting?" asked Duncan, wrinkling his nose.

"I'll tell you all about it later."

"You can tell them now, if you want," said Broxholm. "Kreeblim and I must go in for a meeting with the Council. You'll have some time while we're gone."

With that, the two of them disappeared through the transcendental elevator.

"All right, Peter, give," said Susan.

"Beg pardon?" I asked innocently.

But you know all that part. I told her and Duncan the same story I've just told you.

About the time we were done, Broxholm and Kreeblim returned. "The Council will see you now," said Kreeblim, her nose waving in front of her.

Nervous, excited, terrified, we followed them through the transcendental elevator to the room

where the images of eight aliens were waiting to give us our instructions.

There was something different about the chamber this time. Floating in the center of it was a huge, holographic image of the earth. Think of the globe you have in your classroom. Now imagine it eight feet across, created in perfect detail.

I felt Susan's hand slip into mine. "It's so beautiful," she whispered.

I didn't say anything. From out in space, the planet *was* beautiful. But I knew what was happening back on the surface, what people were doing to each other.

What would happen to *us* when we went back down there? Could we find some way to convince the aliens not to destroy it?

Suddenly, I realized Duncan was standing close to me. To my surprise, he slipped his arm around my shoulder. "We can do it, Peter," he whispered.

I nodded, still staring at the image before us, the image of Earth, the planet I had abandoned, and now must try to save.

My home.

MY TEACHER

Flunked THE Planet

For today's 40,000...
and tomorrow's
and the next day's
until it is finally over

CHAPTER ONE

"Nikka, Nikka, Flexxim Puspa!"

Broxholm's orange eyes were glowing. The leathery, lime-green skin of his face was stretched tight in a look that I could not interpret. The viewscreen behind him showed an image of the Earth, floating in the dark glory of space.

Broxholm pointed to a red button that glowed more brightly than his eyes. "This is it," he said. "*The* button."

My throat was dry. "What would happen if you pushed it?"

His lipless mouth pulled back in something like a smile, revealing rounded, purplish teeth. "Nothing. At least, not now. It takes a complex series of secret commands to activate it."

"And if that series of commands is used?" asked Susan Simmons, who was standing beside me.

Broxholm turned and gazed at the image of Earth. "Stardust," he whispered.

"Whoa!" said Duncan Dougal. "Major bummer!"

Another being entered the chamber. Turning, I

1

saw Kreeblim, the alien who had fried Duncan's brain and made him super-smart. Her lavender hair, thick as worms, was writhing around her head. "The council is ready to see us," she said, gesturing over her shoulder with her long, three-pronged nose.

I swallowed. The Interplanetary Council was trying to decide how to handle what they called "the Earth Question"—which was basically, "What do we do with the only species on ten thousand planets that is bright enough to figure out space travel, yet dumb enough to have wars?"

That species was human beings, of course, and I didn't much care for any of the aliens' current plans, which I had explained to Susan and Duncan earlier that night when I told them the story of my experiences since I had gone into space with Broxholm.

"If we start with the least nasty option and work up," I had said, "then Plan A calls for the aliens to leave us alone for now."

"That's not so bad!" Susan had said.

"Unfortunately, most of the aliens who favor it do so because they figure if they leave us alone, we'll destroy ourselves before we make it into space. That way the problem is solved, and they don't have to feel guilty."

"That *stinks!*" Duncan had cried.

"Agreed. Now, the aliens who support what

2

we'll call Plan B would like to take over the planet."

Susan's eyes had widened. "An alien invasion, just like we feared from the beginning!"

"Not quite. This group wants to fix things. They would cure diseases, stop wars, end poverty, that kind of thing."

Duncan had blinked in surprise. "Sounds great!"

"It would be, except they'll only do it if we give them total control of the planet."

Duncan had started to ask why, then nodded. "They're afraid once they give us their technology we'll use it against them."

"You've got it," I'd said, reminding myself not to be surprised when Duncan figured things out.

"So what's the third option?" Susan had asked.

"Plan C: restrict us to our own solar system, either by sabotaging our science so we never develop faster-than-light travel, or by setting up a military blockade."

Since I have always believed it is our destiny to go to the stars, I hated that idea more than I can tell you.

"Most aliens think that wouldn't work," I had continued. "They figure sooner or later we'd get out anyway. So we have Plan D—D for destruction, you might say. The group supporting this wants to blow us up now, before we can get into space and really make trouble. They believe if we make it out of the solar system, the final cost in lives and destruction will be *far* greater than if they simply wipe us out today. They look at us the way we would look at a group of monkeys that accidentally learned to make atomic bombs: interesting, but too dangerous to be allowed to live."

The bad news was, the aliens seemed to be leaning toward Plan D. The good news was, they were going to let us try to change their minds.

We followed Kreeblim to the wall. She had her pet poot—which was also *named* Poot, for reasons I didn't understand—riding on her shoulder. Poot was sort of an alien slug that oozed and changed shape. I had noticed that Duncan seemed to be very fond of it. I guess it was fond of Duncan, too, since when it noticed him it raised a blob of itself and cried, "Poot!"

Kreeblim stopped in front of a large circle. Mounted in the wall next to it were twelve rows of multicolored marbles. She punched six of the marbles. The circle turned blue.

This was what the aliens call a transcendental elevator. It could transport beings from one place to another instantly—which was just as well, since the *New Jersey* (that was the spaceship we were on) had thousands of miles of corridors.

I followed Kreeblim through the circle and into the meeting chamber of the Interplanetary Council.

Susan gasped when she came in behind me. I didn't blame her. Each of the eight beings on the council came from a different world. Seeing them all together was plenty strange.

Actually, what we were *seeing* were holographic projections of the council members. The council members themselves remained on their own worlds. However, the three-dimensional images were so realistic, I rarely thought about that.

First to speak was an alien who looked like a pile of red seaweed with thick green stalks growing out of the top. It made a series of popping, bubbling sounds, then wiggled the squishy-looking pods that dangled from the end of each stalk to indicate that what it had said was a question.

I understood the gesture because the aliens had installed a Universal Translator in my brain, and it interpreted whatever any of them said. In turn, I was to translate their sounds (and gestures) for Susan and Duncan.

I turned to Susan. Her hair, usually blond, had a green tint from the odd light of the chamber. Susan is very pretty by Earth standards, but I had seen so many versions of beauty since I joined the aliens I didn't think about that much now. "He wants to know if you understand why you are here," I said.

"I do," she replied, speaking directly to Red Seaweed. "Peter told me all about it."

"And do you accept this task?"

Susan took so long to answer that I began to fear that the alien might get upset. I understood; it was a big job. But even so ... I gave her a nudge.

"I accept!" she said, more loudly than I expected.

"And you, Duncan Dougal?" asked an alien who looked more like a shadow than anything real and solid. It spoke by changing the way light reflected from its body.

Duncan's round face was serious. It was hard for me to imagine a kid who had bullied his way through grade school, a kid who appeared to have all the sensitivity of a brick, being responsible for the survival of the planet. But I was prejudiced. Duncan had been picking on me—and everyone else in our class—for so long that it was hard to remember how different he was now that the aliens had unleashed his natural intelligence by frying his brain.

When I translated the question, Duncan nodded. "I accept," he said solemnly.

"And you, Krepta?" asked a tall, sea-green alien.

I hesitated for only a moment. After all, the mission had been partly my idea. "I accept," I said. Though I meant to say it proudly, my voice came out sounding small and scared.

Next to speak was a purple alien whose long tentacles stretched across a silvery rack. A nozzle mounted above the rack sprayed lavender mist over the tentacles, keeping them slick and shiny.

"Broxholm ign Gnarx Erxxen xax Scradzz?" it asked.

That mouthful of syllables represented Broxholm's full name, including his family group (Gnarx Erxxen) and his planet (Scradzz). Broxholm was standing behind me. I turned to look at him. Putting a hand on my shoulder, he wrinkled his high, green forehead—his way of signaling agreement.

The final member of our party to be sworn in was Kreeblim. Her thick lavender hair was rippling with so many conflicting emotions she looked as if she had a colony of confused worms climbing out of her head. I began to wonder if she had changed her mind. But after a moment she closed her third eye, the one in the middle of her forehead, and said, "I accept."

The council didn't ask us to swear on a holy book or anything; the aliens expect that if you say you'll do something, you'll do it. Only I wasn't entirely sure what we had just said we would do.

Basically, they had given us the last three weeks of October to put together a report on the state of Earth and its people.

But what was supposed to be in the report? How could we make them think better of us? At the moment, the aliens viewed us the way you and I look at flu germs—insignificant, yet nasty and dangerous. Or worse. I think they considered all of humanity as a sickness threatening to overtake the galaxy if something wasn't done about us.

"The newcomers will need translators," said a large, batlike alien who dangled from the ceiling in a sling. Its voice, which I had not heard before, was like nails scraping over concrete. I could feel it in my spine.

After Susan and Duncan took their hands away from their ears, I translated the alien's screech. Duncan looked puzzled. "Why do we need translators to go back to Earth?"

"Because your planet, which has yet to figure out the benefit of true communication, has hundreds of different languages," screeched the batlike alien.

The other aliens made sounds of sorrow and disapproval at our backward ways.

When I explained Bat-thing's answer, Duncan's eyes lit up. "You mean these translators will let us understand any language on *Earth?*" he cried eagerly.

"They would hardly be Universal Translators if they didn't," said Red Seaweed, adding a gesture that meant something like, "Is water wet?"

"Wow!" said Duncan. "This is going to be great!" Suddenly his smile faded. The blood drained from his face. "Wait a minute," he said, his voice quavering. "Are you going to do brain surgery on me?"

In my opinion, brain surgery on the old Duncan would have been a good idea. He'd had nothing to lose, and it might have improved things. But now that I had been inside his brain a couple of times (as a result of being hooked into some alien communication machines), I understood why he was so upset. Since the aliens had fried the thing, it was pretty amazing. I wouldn't have wanted to take a chance with it, either.

I was trying to decide whether to tease Duncan or reassure him when a wave of dizziness swept over me. My own brain felt as if it had come loose inside my skull and begun to spin.

"Nikka, nikka, flexxim puspa!" I cried.

As I was wondering where the words had come from, everything went black, and I collapsed in a heap on the floor.

CHAPTER TWO

Long Division

Weird images seemed to crawl through my mind: exploding television sets, vast sea creatures, things being cut in half, things being put together. I felt big. I felt tiny. I felt connected to something huge. I was swimming in an ocean that wasn't made of water, but of—I don't know. Electricity, maybe, though that idea was too weird to hold onto.

Ahead of me was a wall. I had to get past it. But how? Knock it down? Go under it? Swim right through it?

I didn't know. I only knew that something terribly important was waiting on the other side.

Before I could find a way past the wall I heard Susan calling me. Duncan took my hand, and *snap!* I was out of the dream (the vision, whatever). Opening my eyes, I saw four faces—two human, two alien—staring at me with grave concern.

"Peter, what happened?" asked Susan.

I shook my head. "I don't know," I said, thinking how good it was to see her face.

"What was that thing you said?" Duncan asked. "What did it mean?"

I must have looked blank.

"You know, that thing about 'Nikka, nikka, flexxim puspa.' "

Suddenly I remembered the words. Though they hadn't made sense when they first came out of my mouth, I understood them now. They were in the language of Hoo-Lan, the little blue alien who had become my teacher on board the ship. It was Hoo-Lan who had named me Krepta. I was very fond of him. I was also very sad when I thought of him, since he was now in a coma, and no one knew for sure if he would live or not.

Even worse, what had driven him into the coma was trying to make a telepathic link with *my* mind.

"Well?" asked Duncan.

"They mean, approximately, 'One for all and all for one,' " said Broxholm before I could answer.

It was Duncan's turn to look confused. "That's the motto of the Three Musketeers."

I thought: *I really do have to get used to the fact that Duncan knows things like that.* Then I decided I could get used to it later. The first thing I needed to figure out was why I had been quoting a phrase from a French novel in an alien language.

"Can you stand, Krepta?" asked Kreeblim gently.

I had known her only a few hours; I was pleased to hear how kind her voice could be.

"I think so," I said.

"Is the boy all right?" asked Red Seaweed as Susan and Duncan helped me up.

"I'm fine," I muttered. "Just a little woozy."

Actually, I wasn't sure *how* I was. Only I didn't say that, for fear I would be taken off the mission.

"I believe he needs some rest," said Broxholm. Considering what I had been through in the last twenty-four hours, this made sense.

"He can relax in his room while the others receive their translators," said the purple alien.

Duncan was looking more and more nervous. Finally he turned to Kreeblim and said, "Do you suppose I could take the poot with me?"

Kreeblim paused, then pulled the glowing, jellylike blob from her shoulder.

"Poot!" it said, sticking out a couple of eyestalks.

Kreeblim looked at Duncan. "You really do like Poot, don't you?"

Duncan nodded.

Kreeblim seemed to be thinking. At last she grasped the slug firmly in both hands. Then she yanked her arms sideways, pulling the poot like a piece of taffy.

"Stop!" screamed Duncan.

The poot stretched until it was about three feet long. *"Pooooot!"* it cried. *"P-O-O-O-O-O-T!"*

Then it snapped in half.

"What did you do that for?" asked Duncan, his voice quavering.

"I thought you might like a poot of your own," said Kreeblim. She sounded puzzled by Duncan's reaction.

Duncan blinked. Each of Kreeblim's outstretched hands held a poot identical to the one she had pulled off her shoulder, but only half the size. Was one poot the parent and one the child? Or were they both the same poot, now living in two bodies? It was very confusing.

Duncan was pale. "Did you hurt it?" he asked, his voice trembling.

"Not badly," said Kreeblim. "But the extension of life always involves some pain. Pick one."

"Pain or life?" asked Duncan, sounding confused.

"No, pick a poot," she replied, exasperated.

Duncan hesitated, then reached forward and took the small poot that lay quivering in Kreeblim's left hand. "Thank you," he said in a voice that sounded like he was far from certain whether he meant it.

"You are most welcome."

Duncan lifted the poot to his shoulder. After a moment it stretched a blob of itself up, patted him on the cheek, and said, "Poot!"

Duncan smiled and seemed to relax a bit.

"Time to go," said Broxholm as he programmed the transcendental elevator to take Susan and Duncan to CrocDoc. I was very fond of CrocDoc (despite the fact that he once *took out* my brain to examine it!) so I went along to say hello.

Susan and Duncan flinched as we entered the room. I couldn't blame them. CrocDoc was nearly seven feet tall, and looked like a human version of a red crocodile.

"Don't worry," I whispered to Susan. "He's a very good being."

She nodded, but didn't relax.

"Greetings, Krepta," said CrocDoc, displaying his teeth. "May the wisdom of the egg be with you."

"Greetings, Fixer-of-Bodies," I replied, touching my forehead in a gesture of respect. Then I translated for him as he asked Susan and Duncan to climb onto his operating tables.

"I'll see you guys later," I said once they were settled. Leaning close to Susan, I added in a whisper, "Don't worry."

Then I turned to Duncan. "Have fun!" I said cheerfully.

Duncan squeezed his poot, which was still clinging to his shoulder.

I felt a brief wave of dizziness. I knew I should

go to my room to rest, but I decided to visit Hoo-Lan instead.

I had two reasons for this. First, I was terrified that he might die before we finished our mission; if so, this would be the last chance I would ever have to see him. Second, even though he was in a coma, I suspected he was somehow connected to what had happened to me in the council chamber.

I took out my URAT, which Hoo-Lan had given to me the day I met him. A URAT (Universal Reader and Translator) is like a pocket computer, but with more information plugged into it than you can begin to imagine. Flipping it open, I requested the code for Hoo-Lan's room. The screen displayed a pattern of colors. I punched the pattern into the keypad of CrocDoc's transcendental elevator.

When the elevator was ready, I stepped through the wall.

My teacher's little blue body was floating in the center of a nearly invisible bubble. The bubble was a fancy version of the force fields Broxholm and Kreeblim had used to imprison Ms. Schwartz and Duncan. I call it fancy because it was keeping track of everything from Hoo-Lan's temperature to the electrical activity in his brain.

Walking to the bubble, I stared through its clear, curved side. It was strange to see Hoo-Lan, who was one of the liveliest beings I had ever

17

met, lying so still and quiet. His thick white mustache drooped limply beneath his big nose, and his huge eyes were closed. He was glowing, as he had been when he fell into the coma, but the glow was so faint it could barely be seen. I kept thinking of a dying firefly.

I asked the URAT a question. When it gave me the okay, I placed my hands against the bubble.

Nothing. No sense of communication, as Susan and I had felt when we touched the force field that held Ms. Schwartz. But maybe that was good, considering what had put Hoo-Lan here to begin with.

What is so awful about the human brain that it could do this to him? I wondered. I leaned my head against the bubble, trying not to cry.

To my surprise, Hoo-Lan opened one eye.

Opened it, then closed it. Very slowly. That was all.

It took me weeks to figure out what he had just done.

CHAPTER THREE

Big Julie

Seconds after Hoo-Lan opened and closed his eye, another alien came through the wall. This alien—I would say "he" or "she" but you can't always tell with these beings—had a beetlelike shell on its back, and more arms and legs (or whatever) in front than I could count.

"Greetings, Krepta," it said in a language that seemed to consist mostly of clicks.

"Greetings," I replied.

The alien scuttled to Hoo-Lan's bubble. "We registered a small movement."

"He opened one eye," I replied, lowering and raising my own left eyelid in demonstration.

The bug-being waved its antennae. "That's the most he's done since we put him here!" it clicked. "He must have been aware of your arrival."

That made me feel good—though I was still feeling guilty about whether my brain had driven Hoo-Lan into the coma in the first place.

I watched the bug-being putter around for a bit, then decided to go to my room. As I stepped through the wall a ball of red fur dropped from the ceiling to my shoulder. I jumped in surprise, then relaxed as the furball started to chitter.

"Hi, Murgatroyd," I said. Murgatroyd was a skimml. He had been given to me by Fleef and Gurk, two aliens I'd met my first day on the *New Jersey*, as a kind of get-well present after CrocDoc had taken out my brain.

"They're squishy," Gurk had said, squeezing the skimml so hard that red fur had bulged from the top and bottom of his brown fist.

"Lots of fur, no bones," Fleef had explained.

I gave Murgatroyd a squeeze now. He began to chitter more loudly than before. (He *loved* being squished.) Cuddling him to my chest, I whispered, "I think you'd better stay here, fella. I'm not sure what's going to happen down there."

I used my URAT to send a note to Fleef, asking her to take care of Murgatroyd while I was gone. Then I started to pack.

Fifteen minutes later I had stowed everything I wanted in a knapsack I ordered from the synthesizer. Knowing it would be a while before Susan and Duncan were ready to go, I called up a program about undersea life on Hoo-Lan's planet. But even watching three-dimensional sea creatures swim through the middle of my room couldn't take my mind off what we were facing. It was almost a relief when Broxholm walked through my wall and said, "Time to go."

I followed him to the departure chamber. Duncan, Susan, and Kreeblim were already there.

No one else came to tell us good-bye and good luck.

No brass band played to send us on our heroic mission. But that was no surprise, given Broxholm's feelings about band music.

Besides, the aliens didn't think what we were doing was all that heroic. They had given us a last chance before they decided our fate, and we were just doing something that ought to be done.

I glanced around at the ship, then closed my eyes and stepped into the blue light.

We materialized in a kitchen. The house we were in belonged to Betty Lou Karpou, which was Kreeblim's Earth identity. Only something had changed in the few hours since we had left it.

At first, I couldn't figure out what it was.

Then I realized that I could hear someone breathing.

Someone who wasn't a member of our group.

Someone who was very, *very* big.

I glanced at Broxholm. He looked wary. Remembering how sensitive his ears were, I guessed that he had picked up the sound of the breathing right away. As I watched, Kreeblim caught the expression on his face. "What is it, Broxholm?" she asked.

Before he could answer, she noticed the sound, too. Her eyes went wide, and she said a word nearly unpronounceable for a human tongue. It came from deep in her throat, and about the best I can do to represent it is, "Uhrbhighgjououol-lee."

Broxholm wrinkled his brow in affirmation.

Duncan wrinkled his brow, too, but in his case it indicated puzzlement. "Did you say 'You're Big Julie'?"

Broxholm showed the tiniest bit of amusement. "That's not exactly what she said, but for your purposes, it's close enough."

"Who's Big Julie?" asked Susan.

"I AM!"

The words, spoken in a whisper, rumbled through the floorboards like thunder through a cloud. Duncan screamed and grabbed Susan's arm.

"Who said that?" I asked nervously.

The floor shivered again as the voice whispered, "I DID!"

"Oh, stop it, Uhrbhighgjououol-lee," snapped Kreeblim. "You're frightening our friends."

"THEY FRIGHTEN ME!"

"Broxholm, please tell us what's going on," said Susan.

Broxholm pulled on his nose, which was his way of sighing, and said, "We've been assigned a watchdog." He sounded annoyed.

"What do you mean?" I asked.

"The council doesn't entirely trust Kreeblim and me not to become too fond of you earthlings.

22

So they've sent Uhrbhighgjououol-lee to keep an eye on us, to prevent any such fondness from leading us into a bad decision."

"You mean this guy is here to keep you from going native?" I asked. If our situation hadn't been so serious, I would have thought the idea was pretty funny.

Kreeblim closed her middle eye. "You could put it that way."

Susan frowned. "Well, where is he? Is he some weird creature with no body? Did he sink his molecules into the floor?"

Broxholm showed that hint of amusement again. "Big Julie is hardly a creature without a body," he said mildly. He started to say something else, but his words were interrupted by that deep voice.

"I AM *HERE*," it rumbled. "COME SEE."

Duncan moved closer to me. I gave Broxholm a questioning look.

"It's all right," said Kreeblim. "He won't hurt you. Yet."

"Yet?" asked Susan.

Broxholm showed his purple teeth. "Big Julie does not like earthlings very much. I suspect one reason he was chosen to keep an eye on us is that he is one of the most vocal supporters of the blow-up-Earth-today faction. Even so, you might as well go meet him."

"The breathing sounds like it's coming from

23

down the hall," said Susan. She glanced at Broxholm, who wrinkled his brow in affirmation. Reaching out, she took my hand.

The slow, steady sound of Big Julie's breathing filled the air.

CHAPTER FOUR

Springing Susan

Imagine you're walking down a hall in a house that belongs to an alien. You're scared, but not too scared, because the alien has turned out to be fairly friendly. Still and all, you know this is a pretty weird place.

Filling the air around you, so slow you can hardly make it out, yet unmistakable once you've noticed it, is the sound of incredibly deep breathing—as if someone were trying to take a deep breath, and then couldn't stop, but just kept breathing in, in, in. And then, finally, the seemingly endless exhalation.

"There," I whispered, pointing to a closed door.

Susan nodded. Duncan said nothing, but took a deep breath himself.

We moved closer. I could feel air moving around my feet.

"Should we knock?" Duncan whispered.

"It might sound aggressive," Susan replied.

"Then let's just talk to him," I said. Raising my voice a bit, I called, "May we come in?"

"NO!"

"Maybe we should just go," whispered Duncan.

Before I could answer, the voice spoke again. "YOU CAN'T COME IN BECAUSE YOU CAN'T COME IN. BUT YOU CAN OPEN THE DOOR."

I reached forward, turned the doorknob, and pulled. Then I screamed.

I don't feel bad about that. I bet you would scream, too, if you found yourself face to face with an eyeball taller than you are.

At least I knew why Big Julie had said we couldn't come in. There was no room! His vast body—green and brown, if the bit of flesh I could see at the bottom of the door was any indication—took up every bit of space available on the other side of the door.

"GREETINGS, LITTLE ONES. DID YOU HAVE A GOOD TRIP?"

"What do you care?" asked Susan, her voice bitter.

Big Julie blinked, his eyelid moving so slowly it looked like a shade being pulled over a window, then raised again. The blink made me think of something, something that seemed important. Only I couldn't figure out what it was.

"I HAVE NO GRUDGE AGAINST YOU. IT'S YOUR *SPECIES* THAT TERRIFIES ME."

I didn't want to get into that debate again, so

I decided to change the subject. "How did you get in that room? Did they beam you into it?"

"I CAME DOWN IN PIECES."

"Eeuuw!" cried Duncan. "That's disgusting."

Big Julie's sigh made the floor shake. "ONE OF THE MANY PROBLEMS WITH YOUR PEOPLE IS YOUR DISGUST WITH THE MATTER OF LIFE. LISTEN!"

He belched, which made the walls of the room rattle.

"HEAR THAT? IT'S THE SOUND OF LIFE IN ACTION. PROCESS. BIOLOGY. STOP IT, AND YOU'RE DEAD. HOW CAN IT BE DISGUSTING?"

"It was lovely," I said. "Please tell us more about coming down in pieces."

"WHAT WAS ONE CAN BECOME MANY," he replied. "WHAT WAS MANY CAN BECOME ONE. YOU JUST HAVE TO KNOW HOW TO DO IT."

"What does that mean?" asked Duncan, his curiosity overcoming his fear.

"JUST BECAUSE SOMETHING IS SPLIT DOESN'T MEAN IT'S BEEN DIVIDED."

"Thanks for the clarification," muttered Duncan.

I was trying to figure out what to ask next when Broxholm came down the hall. He stopped in front of Big Julie and touched his forehead in a gesture that my translator told me indicated formal respect, but not friendship. "We need to make some plans," he said. "So if you will excuse us . . ."

"PLAN AWAY," said Big Julie. His voice was jovial, as if he knew that whatever we did, it wouldn't make any difference.

"I don't understand how he can keep an eye on you if he can't leave the room," I said as Broxholm led us back to the kitchen.

"Man, if that guy kept an eye on you, it would squash you flat!" said Duncan.

"Kreeblim and I will have to report back to him on a regular basis," Broxholm explained. "If he suspects we are becoming too involved, he will communicate his worries to the ship, and we will be called back. Also, he can, I suspect, detect anything said within these walls."

"THAT'S RIGHT!"

I was hoping we might sit down and eat when we got back to the kitchen. But as we walked through the door Susan glanced at the clock. "Oh, no!" she cried. "I was supposed to be home half an hour ago!"

With all that had happened in the last several hours, I had completely forgotten that when the evening started she had told her parents she was going to a school dance. She had left the dance to sneak into Kreeblim's house, hoping to find Duncan, and ended up getting dragged into space and having brain surgery. Under the circumstances, I didn't think half an hour late was that bad. Unfortunately, it wasn't the kind of excuse Susan's mother would understand.

"If I don't get home soon, I'll be grounded for life," she groaned.

"Your parents can't ground you," said Duncan. "You have to save the world."

"*You* tell that to my mother," snapped Susan. Suddenly she looked nervous. "You *are* going to let me go home, aren't you?" she asked, turning to Kreeblim.

Kreeblim's lavender hair leaned to the right. "We have to. When I abducted Duncan, people were willing to believe he had run away. They were upset, but not *suspicious*."

Actually, I doubted that anyone except his mother was even upset. I could remember nights when I had prayed that Duncan would run away. Of course, he was different now. But I suspected that not many people had gotten used to that idea.

Kreeblim was still talking. "If *you* were to disappear as well, it could cause a panic. Given the events of last spring, people would connect your disappearance to our work."

She glanced at Broxholm when she said this, twitching her nose sharply to the left. The gesture told me something I hadn't realized before: she was Broxholm's boss! The nose-twitch was a reminder that she thought he had been careless last spring when he had let Susan and the school band overcome him. They had used music, which affects Broxholm ten times worse than finger-nails scraping on a blackboard affects us. (I happen to know that he had had special ear filters installed since that incident.)

That information was passed in less than a second. Kreeblim didn't even pause in what she was saying. "While a panic about your disappearance would not stop us, it would create problems I would rather avoid at the moment."

"So what do we do now?" asked Susan. She sounded cranky, which was unusual for her. I realized she must be very tired.

"To start with, I'll call your home, as Betty Lou Karpou, and tell them it's my fault you're late. I'll say I asked you to help me clean up after the dance and we lost track of time."

Susan smiled. "That ought to work. Mom loves it when I help my teachers."

Kreeblim pulled her poot off her shoulder and handed it to Duncan. He looked at it for a moment, and then held it at arm's length. I think he was afraid it might try to merge with his own poot, which was resting on his shoulder.

Susan recited her number to Kreeblim, who had moved to the phone. She dialed, waited, then spoke quietly and calmly to Mrs. Simmons. After a few minutes she extended the phone to Susan, who talked briefly, then hung up and said, "If you can get me home in half an hour, I'll be safe. Then all we have to do is figure out how to get me free from school for the next month!"

"I've got an idea," said Duncan eagerly.

When everyone looked at him he began to blush. I was surprised; I used to think nothing embarrassed Duncan.

"Yes?" asked Kreeblim, her voice soft and encouraging.

Duncan took a breath. He began rubbing the side of his nose, which my translator told me was a nervous gesture. "What if we told Susan's parents that she just won some kind of travel scholarship?"

"What do you mean?" asked Broxholm.

Duncan shrugged. "Susan is *always* getting awards for being good at something. We could say she sent in an essay and won a trip to Washington, or something like that."

"Not bad," said Kreeblim, closing her middle eye in approval.

It didn't take Broxholm and Kreeblim long to develop Duncan's idea. The nice thing was, they welcomed suggestions from us kids as well. Working together, we decided that Susan had won the Patricia MacDonald Junior High Home Economics Travel Fellowship. Since "Betty Lou Karpou" was the junior high home economics teacher, Kreeblim could tell Susan's parents that she had sponsored Susan in the contest and would accompany her on the trip.

The question was, would Mr. and Mrs. Simmons believe it?

I underestimated the aliens on that matter. After Kreeblim told the Simmonses that the real reason they were late was that they had just gotten this *fabulous* news about Susan's scholarship, Broxholm and Kreeblim spent the next morning sending telegrams and making phone calls congratulating the Simmonses on their daughter's achievement. "It is children like Susan who give us the hope of a better future—indeed, of any future at all," said the absolutely truthful special-delivery letter the Simmonses received that afternoon.

A similar letter went to Dr. Wilburn, the school principal.

"She made such a fuss over me it was embarrassing!" cried Susan that evening.

I thought, but didn't say, that she ought to be used to it, since teachers had been making a fuss over her for years.

"I had a harder time convincing Dr. Wilburn to give *me* the time off than I did with Susan's parents," growled Kreeblim, her nose lashing from side to side. "I finally had to agree to pay for my own substitute."

"Money's not a problem for you guys, is it?" asked Duncan. He sounded concerned.

Broxholm laughed, a sound like grinding metal. "Money is not the issue. Kreeblim likes to bargain. It's a special skill among her people. She's upset because she couldn't get a better deal on this."

Kreeblim's nose continued its angry movements. "I was working under a severe handicap. Teachers get almost no respect on this world."

"TRULY A SICK PLACE," rumbled Big Julie.

Broxholm wrinkled his brow in agreement. "That was one of the first things that struck me about this planet. I still can't understand why the world's most important job is treated so badly."

I looked at him in surprise. Did he really believe that *teaching* was the world's most important job?

That night Mr. and Mrs. Simmons and Dr. Wilburn drove Susan and "Betty Lou Karpou" to the airport in Hamilton, which was the nearest city to Kennituck Falls. The aliens hadn't wanted to go to all that trouble. But they knew Susan's parents would insist on seeing her off.

What Mr. and Mrs. Simmons *didn't* know was that after the plane landed, their daughter and her "teacher" would take a cab out of Washington, so they could join the alien who had tried to kidnap Susan last spring, and try to save the world.

CHAPTER FIVE

Rumors of War

"Come on," said Broxholm later that night. "They're about to land."

Duncan glanced at the clock on the wall. "I wouldn't be too sure," he said, shifting his poot from one shoulder to the other. "Planes are late a lot these days."

I smiled as Broxholm held out his URAT so Duncan could see the screen, which showed Kreeblim in her Betty Lou Karpou disguise. When Duncan's poot saw Kreeblim/Karpou, it lifted its head—at least the portion it was using for its head at the moment—and cried, "Poot! Poot, poot, poot!"

(Kreeblim's own poot was in a Tupperware container in the refrigerator, which was where she kept it when she was away.)

Kreeblim smiled, then mouthed the words, "Hello, Duncan."

Duncan blinked. "She can see me?"

Broxholm wrinkled his brow yes. "We linked URATs before she left for the airport. She could even speak to you, if not for the fact that she doesn't want to arouse suspicion."

"Easier than using a phone, I suppose," muttered Duncan. He was trying not to seem too surprised by things—though how *I* knew that I wasn't quite sure.

"Anyway," continued Broxholm, "Kreeblim says they will be landing soon. Therefore, we should leave."

We followed Broxholm to Kreeblim's cellar. Like his own cellar, this had a secret trapdoor leading to a second cellar—an enormous, glowing, egg-shaped chamber where Kreeblim kept what most people would call her flying saucer. I don't like that term; it sounds hokey. But if I described the vehicle to people—described the shape, the lights, the way it moved—they would just nod and say, "Oh, right! A flying saucer!" So I might as well call it that and get it over with.

Our seats were in a bubble compartment that let us see our surroundings, though at the moment that meant nothing more than a curved, glowing wall.

Broxholm touched a yellow half-sphere on the control panel, then spoke a word deep in his throat. The ship began to move forward. Duncan gasped as we lifted into the air. I figured he was afraid we were going to crash into the ceiling. I understood the feeling: I had felt it myself the night I went off with Broxholm. But there was no need to worry. Kreeblim's backyard tilted up like a giant trapdoor and we shot safely into the night sky.

Broxholm manipulated two of the control spheres. "This will shield us from radar detection," he said.

Minutes later we were flying over Washington, D.C., a trip that would have taken hours in a jet plane. We were so high that Washington and Baltimore were nothing more than smears of light across the land beneath us.

"I thought you might like to see that," said Broxholm, gesturing to the lights. He touched the control panel again. We shot forward, then began to fall almost straight down.

Sometimes your brain knows things that your body doesn't believe. For example, I was sure Broxholm was in control of the ship. But it was all I could do to keep from screaming when I saw the ground rushing toward us.

Long before we would have hit, he began to slow our fall. Five minutes later we made a gentle landing in a deserted field.

"How far are we from the city?" I asked as we climbed out of the saucer.

"About sixty miles," said Broxholm. He stretched out on the grass and began to gaze at the sky, which was clear and filled with stars.

I lay down next to him. The stars seemed different to me now that I knew more of what was out there, knew that intelligent beings on ten thousand worlds were trying to decide what to do about us.

After a while Broxholm made one of his nose-sighs. I wondered if he was missing his home.

A light breeze whispered through my hair. Bugs were singing, and bats zipped through the darkness overhead. A light dew covered the grass. The dew was cool against my hands, which I had crossed behind my head. It was a good night. I thought: *if I had ever been able to share a time like this with my father, would I have gone off with Broxholm?* I turned to Broxholm and started to say something, but decided not to.

After about forty-five minutes I heard a car in the distance. It came closer, stopped for a few minutes, then drove on. Broxholm glanced at his URAT. "That's them."

Soon I saw Susan and Kreeblim walking across the field. "Poot!" cried Duncan's poot, stretching a pair of eyestalks toward Kreeblim.

A shooting star streaked through the sky above us.

Kreeblim's saucer was fast; less than twenty minutes after she and Susan joined us we were in Arizona, where the five of us sat on the edge of a cliff, sharing peanut butter sandwiches, crisp apples, and some blobby things that Kreeblim called fimflits.

My first bite of fimflits made my tongue think

it had died and gone to heaven. When I asked about them, Kreeblim told me they were a kind of fungus people ate on her home planet.

Then she told us what they grew on.

"Eeuuw!" cried Duncan, spitting a mouthful of fimflit over the edge of the cliff.

I don't want to say ignorance is bliss, but clearly Duncan had been a lot happier before he knew the whole truth about fimflits.

A moment later Kreeblim brushed her hands together, then slapped her cheek three times—a gesture that, on her world, meant it was time to get down to business.

"I think we need to start with an overview," she said, using her nose to pluck a fimflit crumb from her cheek.

"An overview of *what*?" asked Susan. "This may sound stupid, but I'm still not sure exactly what we're doing."

"An overview of the problem. We need to show you the reasons Earth has become such an issue throughout the galaxy before we can start to look for some hope that things can change." Kreeblim hesitated, then added, "You're going to see some things that aren't pretty; things some adults would say are unsuitable for children to know about."

"An odd attitude," said Broxholm, "since a lot of these 'unsuitable' things are happening *to* kids."

"You know, none of this is our fault," said Susan. "We're just kids. Why don't you talk to someone in the government?"

"We've considered it," said Broxholm. "But most of our projections indicate that formal contact between the Planetary League and one or all of your governments would result in a major war here on Earth."

"You mean we'd end up fighting *with each other*?" I asked in surprise.

"Correct," said Kreeblim, swatting a mosquito with her nose.

"That doesn't make any sense," protested Duncan.

Kreeblim made her version of a shrug. "How many of your other wars have made sense? Fear is a very powerful motivator among your people. It prompts them to do senseless things."

That shut us up, until Duncan said, "I've got an idea! Why don't you just fry *everyone's* brains?"

A silver lid flickered over Broxholm's orange eyes—a sign of worried surprise. He looked at Kreeblim. Kreeblim looked back. When neither of them spoke, I sensed bad news coming.

"Duncan," said Kreeblim at last, "come with me. I need to talk to you."

Looking terrified, Duncan got to his feet and followed Kreeblim into the darkness.

41

CHAPTER SIX

What Goes On in the Human Heart?

Broxholm, Susan, and I sat at the edge of the cliff, waiting for Duncan and Kreeblim to return. The star-spangled dome of the sky curved above us. After a while Susan said, "Is the brain-fry going to kill him?"

"Of course not," said Broxholm.

I closed my eyes and said, "But it's not going to last, is it? He's going to get stupid again."

"Duncan was never stupid," Broxholm replied sharply. "He *thought* he was stupid, so he acted that way. As near as I can make out, this is fairly common among your people. Somehow, without ever really intending to, your schools and families conspire to create that effect. It's quite frightening."

I thought about that for a minute. "But the brain-fry *is* going to wear off, right?"

Broxholm did one of those brow-wrinkles that mean yes among his people. "Duncan will go back to being what he was—with one difference. He will know, in a way no one else on your planet understands, what his brain is capable of."

"Is that good or bad?" asked Susan.

Broxholm gave her a questioning look.

"I mean, will it help him use his brain better, or just leave him feeling sad?"

Before Broxholm could answer I heard a shout in the distance. "*Noooooo!* No, I don't want that to happen!"

The cry echoed through the darkness.

I shivered and moved closer to Susan. I could see a tear running down her cheek.

When Duncan and Kreeblim returned, Duncan was pale and trembling. I was amazed that I could feel so much sympathy for him after all he had done to me over the years. Yet the look on his face was so filled with loss that I almost started to cry myself.

My brain has always been my proudest possession. So I should have had some understanding of how he felt. But I could hardly imagine what it would be like to think I was stupid all my life, suddenly gain an incredible ability to use my brain, and then be told I was going to lose that ability.

I only knew that the idea wasn't pretty.

Neither was my awareness that I had been jealous of Duncan's magnified brain power. I understood *that* when I realized that part of me felt happy he was going to lose it. I felt disgusted with myself for thinking that way.

At first, no one knew what to say. Duncan was clutching his poot so tightly that bits of it oozed between his fingers. Kreeblim's wormy hair lay as flat and still as if it had died. (My translator told me that was a sign of great sorrow.)

"Well," said Duncan at last. "We're going to start with an overview of all the things wrong with this stupid planet. Then what do we do? Something equally amusing?"

Kreeblim's nose lashed sideways, a sign she was offended by Duncan's tone. I guess she made allowance for his despair, though, because she spoke calmly. "Once we finish the overview, the real work begins. That's when we start our search for a reason to hope things could be different."

"How do we do that?" Susan asked.

"We meet people—talk to them, try to understand. I'm sure you've realized by now that we've been monitoring Earth's television broadcasts for many years. Studying these shows first alerted us to the danger posed by your planet. However, some of us believe there *must* be more to your people than your television would indicate."

"Space beyond!" cried Broxholm, which seemed to be some sort of religious statement. "If we judged earthlings on the basis of what they've done with television, we'd just blow up the planet and have done with it. How they invented it when they did, I'll never know. They certainly weren't *ready* for it. How a culture can expose their young to such—such—"

He was so upset he couldn't finish his sentence. Instead, he made a gesture with no exact Earth equivalent. The closest translation my implant could provide was something like, "I spit in deep disgust upon your decision to play in your own garbage."

Only the last word wasn't *garbage*.

"Weren't you already meeting people in our school?" asked Duncan after Broxholm had calmed down.

"The study in your school was only a pilot project," said Kreeblim, "a starting point."

"What made you pick our school to begin with?" I asked.

"It's so utterly typical of what people *want* to believe the schools in your country are like," replied Broxholm in a tone of voice that made it clear he had a hard time believing people could be so stupid. "Also, it was an easy place for us to fit into; we had monitored so many television programs about schools just like it that we knew what to expect. We planned to move on to other research soon."

"What happened to that plan?" Susan asked.

"*You,*" Broxholm replied sharply.

"That's not entirely fair, Broxholm," said Kreeblim. Turning to Susan, she added, "But there is a grain of truth in it. You unmasked

Broxholm at about the same time we gathered some alarming information regarding new advances in Earth's science. This combination of events gave the faction pushing for Earth's destruction powerful new arguments."

Susan turned pale.

"I don't get it," said Duncan. "If you have such a great spy system, what do we need this mission for?"

"Our monitoring and translation equipment picks up every bit of information your governments transmit," Broxholm answered. "That's easy. What we *don't* understand is what goes on in the human heart. How can an intelligent species be at war against itself? *That* is the mystery we must solve, the riddle we hope to unravel before the council decides that Earth is too great a menace to be allowed to continue."

"And that is where you come in," said Kreeblim. "Broxholm and I will get us into places—we'll provide disguises, even make you invisible when necessary. But we need *you* to interpret things for us, to- explain the earthling point of view. After all, your way of thinking is as alien to us as ours is to you."

"All we're really looking for," added Broxholm, "is hope; a reason to believe things aren't as bad as they look. Or that they could get better. Maybe even just an *explanation* for how things

46

got this way. If we can figure *that* out, perhaps we can find a cure."

"But why *us?*" asked Duncan. "Couldn't grown-ups tell you more about why things are the way they are?"

Kreeblim flapped her nose no. "Few adults could approach this with clear vision. Once adults accept things as they are, most of them stop seeing how they could be different. You three stand at the edge of usefulness—old enough to serve as guides, young enough not to be blinded by familiarity."

She stood and began to walk toward the saucer. The rest of us followed her. Moments later we were flying over the Grand Canyon. I had never been there—my father and I had never taken a trip together that I could remember. I'd seen pictures of it, of course, but that's not the same thing. Pictures can't tell you what it *feels* like to be there.

Kreeblim touched the control panel. The saucer stopped and hung in midair above the canyon. Its depth, its vastness looked both majestic and mysterious in the light of the full moon. For some reason it made me think of the strange vision I had experienced when I fainted in the council chamber.

For some reason it made me start to cry.

"Your planet has some wonderful things," said

Broxholm just before Kreeblim sent us speeding into the night again.

We weren't in the dark for long. Her little ship was so fast it could go halfway around the world, from darkness to daylight, in a matter of minutes. She took us to Asia, though as Broxholm said, we could have gone almost anywhere—Africa, Central America, Europe—and seen the same thing.

"Prepare yourselves," Kreeblim said, slowing the ship until it was barely moving. "This is the heart of the problem. And it isn't pretty."

CHAPTER SEVEN

A Problem Written in Blood

I'd seen people die on television, of course—
sometimes in made-up stories, sometimes on the
news. Let me tell you, it's not the same as seeing
it *happen*, not the same as actually watching people shoot each other, watching flesh rip and blood
spurt as men, women, and children fall, never to
rise again.

Not the same at all.

As I stared at the battle I remembered Broxholm telling me that it had been over three thousand years since any other intelligent species in
the galaxy had had a war, and I understood why
the aliens were so frightened of us.

I glanced at my friend. His skin, usually a deep
lime-green, was an off-yellow that told me he felt
very ill.

"Perhaps it *would* be better to put an end to
this," he whispered, his voice thick with sorrow.
"We *cannot* allow such a sickness to escape into
the galaxy at large."

I understood what he meant. Trying not to cry,
I watched as Duncan, his face grim, pressed his

poot against his shoulder. I remembered him telling me that he had never been allowed to have a teddy bear, because his father thought it would make him a sissy. I wished I had brought Murgatroyd; I could have used something to hold onto myself.

Another round of gunfire shook the air beneath us. More blood, more screams. Suddenly Susan grabbed my arm. "What's *he* doing?" she whispered.

Looking in the direction she pointed, I saw a man crawling across the line of fire. Then I spotted his goal. He was trying to rescue a boy, not much older than me, who had been wounded and couldn't get away from the fighting.

It was terrible to watch. I felt my muscles begin to tense, as if somehow I could lend the man strength. Nearer he crept, and nearer. Then, when he was less than a yard from the boy, a bomb landed. Mud erupted into the air.

Man and boy were gone.

I could feel Susan shaking. "We didn't even know which side they were on! Were they good guys or bad guys?"

I closed my eyes, unable to answer.

Susan turned to Kreeblim. "Please take us out of here."

"We can go," said Kreeblim. "But it won't end the battle."

*   *   *

Our next stop was in South America. The aliens flew us over a vast section of charred, black land, where smoke curled from the remains of fallen trees. My first thought was that this was the aftermath of some enormous forest fire.

"I can't believe people are so careless," I muttered.

"Careless?" asked Broxholm. "This was no accident."

Then he explained that we were looking at a section of Amazon rain forest that had been burned to clear grazing land for cattle.

"You seem to be at war against the planet itself," said Kreeblim after she had shown us a Russian river thick with poisonous chemicals and an American forest brown from acid rain. The tone in her voice told me she found the idea almost impossible to understand. "It's as if there is some secret rage in your species, some hidden pain that is driving you to destroy the things around you."

Broxholm echoed her confusion. "To treat your planet this way—it's like being at war with your own body."

Susan, Duncan, and I were silent. What could we say?

Moments later we were flying above Africa. Kreeblim shielded the ship so that it could not be seen. As she brought it down for a landing, Broxholm pulled three small chains from a compartment located beneath the control panel. From each chain dangled a metal sphere. One by one, he hung the chains over our heads. Then he took a small box from the same compartment. It had a yellow button on the top.

Broxholm pushed the button.

"Hey!" cried Duncan. "Where did everyone go?"

I laughed. It didn't take Duncan long to see (or not see, so to speak) his mistake.

"Oh, wow! We're invisible! How did you do *that*?"

"You can access the technical details through the computer in Kreeblim's house," said Broxholm. "Peter will show you how."

I started to object, then realized I didn't really mind showing Duncan how to get into the computer.

"We want to go up close for this observation," said Kreeblim, "and we want to do it unseen. However, we also need to be able to communicate. Broxholm, if you would refocus us for a moment . . ."

Suddenly we were all visible again.

"Take one of these," said Kreeblim, handing each of us a V-shaped strap. The straps had small, squishy balls at their upper ends, and dime-sized circles made of some sticky fabric at the bottom. "Tuck the receivers into your ears," she said, demonstrating with her own strap, "then attach the transmitter to your throat."

The balls were the receivers, the sticky patch was the transmitter. I pressed the patch lightly against my throat and felt it stick to my skin.

"These will let us speak to each other without being heard by anyone else," said Kreeblim. "The slide on the right strap sets the volume at which you hear what we say. Start at about halfway, then adjust it as you please. Tap the throat patch twice to turn the device on, three times to turn it off."

After we had fiddled with our devices a bit, I heard Kreeblim ask, "How does this sound?"

I blinked. She had moved her lips in silence. Yet her words came clearly through the little receivers in my ears.

"If you whisper without speaking aloud, the throat patch will pick up the vibrations and broadcast them," Broxholm explained.

"LIKE THIS?" asked Duncan.

I felt as if someone had bellowed directly in my ear.

Broxholm flinched, and closed his eyes in pain. *"No, not like that!"* he whispered fiercely.

Duncan looked crushed. He started to apologize, then stopped, afraid of messing up again.

"Remove the patch from your throat," said Kreeblim.

Duncan did as she instructed.

"All of you," she said, looking at me and Susan.

We did the same thing.

"I should have given you a chance to practice first," said Kreeblim. "It's not really your fault, Duncan."

He nodded, but I could tell he felt bad anyway. It was kind of sad. The old Duncan would have thought what he had just done was funny.

Or would he?

Suddenly I realized he might simply have *pretended* to think it was funny. I wondered if Duncan had always been sensitive about his mistakes.

"Try to speak without letting any sound come out," said Broxholm.

We all practiced for a bit. When we thought we had it right, they let us reattach the throat patches.

"How's this?" I asked, in a voice softer than a whisper.

Kreeblim smiled and nodded. "Just right," she replied directly in my ear.

We practiced a little longer, then stepped from the ship, invisible and silent. I gasped. If fimflits had made my tongue think it had died and gone to heaven, what I saw now made my *heart* feel like it had died and gone to hell.

CHAPTER EIGHT

The Forty Thousand

The sun was hot, the land was dry, and the people were dying. Not rapidly, as they had in the war zone. Slowly.

Very slowly.

We were standing outside a refugee camp where people had come in search of food. But there was no food, or at least not enough to make a difference.

I don't know how to write about this, how to explain it to you. Even now my fingers tremble and my eyes blur with tears. I remember what Kreeblim said to Susan: "You're going to see some things that aren't pretty; things some adults would say are unsuitable for children to know about."

I thought about that as I stood near a fence, staring at a girl. If it was unsuitable for me to know what was happening to her, what was it for her to have to live with it? Was that suitable?

Though the girl was about my age, I'd be surprised if she weighed fifty pounds. I made a circle with my thumb and forefinger. I couldn't see it, because I was invisible, but I could tell that I could have made it around her upper arm and had room to spare. Her face was gaunt, her eyes large. She walked like an old woman.

"Why did you bring us here?" demanded Susan. She was speaking to the aliens, not me, but the transmitter at her throat sent her words directly into my ears. Even though she hadn't spoken aloud, her voice was thick with emotion.

"The first step is to identify the problem," replied Broxholm.

I decided to follow the girl. She came to a tent where two younger children sat, both as skinny as she was. The youngest—it was hard to tell his age—was naked. His arms were like sticks, but his belly was round. He stared into the distance like someone who was already dead.

The girl spoke. I was momentarily startled at understanding her, until I remembered that our Universal Translators could interpret Earth languages.

"No food today," was all she said.

The other two didn't say anything, didn't cry, didn't complain, and I knew it was because they had no hope. They were expecting nothing, and it was no surprise when nothing was what they got.

I realized that I had never been hungry in my life. I had thought I was hungry lots of times. I had been mad at my father because he hadn't bothered to shop, because all we had in the house was food I didn't care for. But I had had no idea what real hunger was all about.

"Eat your food, there are children starving in Ethiopia," parents tell kids. We joke about it, because we know the food we don't eat won't do those kids any good. But it didn't feel like a joke now. Once when I was connected to Duncan's brain I had found a memory of how he had hidden in the dumpster behind our school. Now I thought: *the trash he had been wallowing in could have saved these kids' lives.*

I walked on, coming to a tent where two doctors, a man and a woman, were working. People sat, stood, lay on the ground, waiting to see them. The doctors looked tired.

"What am I doing here?" whispered the male doctor as he stuck a needle into an arm that was more bone than flesh. "I don't have to be here. Why am I doing this?"

I was startled to realize that he was an American.

"You can go home anytime," said the woman, her voice soft, sad.

The man shook his head. "This would be the only thing I could think of."

"I know," said the woman.

They went back to their work.

On the far side of the tent I saw a young woman sitting beneath a ragged, drooping tree.

The woman was holding a baby to her breast, which was as flat and wrinkled as a crumpled paper bag. She had no milk. I looked at her for a long time.

After a while she lowered the baby into her lap and closed her eyes. Her shoulders began to shake.

That was when I realized the baby was dead.

I turned and ran.

"Why did you take us there?" demanded Susan when we were back on the ship. Her face was pale, her cheeks moist with tears that kept coming, no matter how many times she wiped her eyes. She was as angry as I have ever seen her.

"Because we want you to explain it to us," said Broxholm.

"Forget explaining it," said Susan. "Why don't *you* do something about it?"

Broxholm looked at her, his orange eyes glowing in astonishment. "What do you mean?"

"Stop it. *Fix it!* You could feed those people, couldn't you?"

"Why should we?" asked Broxholm, genuinely puzzled.

"Because it's so terrible."

"Yes, but why should *we* stop it when you can do it yourselves?"

"But we can't. We just don't have enough food

for everyone!" Susan's voice began to falter. "Do we?"

Kreeblim looked at Broxholm. He nodded, and she sent the saucer into the air. Soon we were hovering over a large building, not that far from where we had seen the starving people. Kreeblim made some adjustments to the control panel, then said, "Turn around."

The center of the floor contained a holographic image, a three-dimensional picture of the warehouse below us.

"Watch," said Broxholm.

Kreeblim made another adjustment. The image shifted as the walls of the building vanished, revealing what was inside.

It was food. Enormous amounts of food.

The aliens spent the next hour taking us around the world, showing us place after place where vast amounts of food were stored. We saw mountains of food that weren't being used, enough for every hungry person on the planet.

"All right, I believe you," said Susan finally.

"You really didn't know, did you?" asked Broxholm in astonishment.

"I knew," said Duncan.

I looked at him in surprise. It had been a long time since he had spoken.

"I know a lot of things," he said. His voice sounded haunted. "I tried to tell our government about it, but they wouldn't listen. At first, I thought it was because they didn't understand. I don't believe that anymore. I believe that for some reason they're convinced it *can't* be helped. But I can't understand why." He put his hands on either side of his head. "For the time being I am one of the smartest people in the world. Possibly the very smartest. Yet I can't make any sense out of what's going on down there."

Kreeblim flapped her nose in dismay. "It has us baffled as well," she said. "But it *has* to be connected to the whole situation. There must be a reason why you can let people starve when there is enough to go around."

"But it's not that *many*, is it?" asked Susan desperately. I could tell she was aching to believe that what we had seen was some weird accident, a mistake.

"Forty thousand," said Duncan. His eyes were closed, as if he were reading from a page inside his head.

"What?" asked Susan.

"Forty thousand," he repeated. "That's how many kids die every day from things that could be changed if we, all of us, the people of Earth, decided they should be."

I took in a sharp breath; forty thousand was more than twice the population of Kennituck Falls.

"Forty thousand a day," continued Duncan relentlessly. "That's a quarter of a million a week.

Over a million a month. Nearly fifteen million a year. They die from not having vaccinations that cost less than a dollar apiece. They die from dirty wells and lack of food. They die from the fact that people don't care, at least, not enough to change it."

Duncan sat frozen, as if in a trance. Tears leaked from beneath his lowered eyelids, cutting paths through the dust of the camp that still covered his cheeks. His voice was like the voice of God, listing our sins.

"Last year fourteen million children died because we earthlings chose to spend our money elsewhere. It happened the year before, too. And we're going to let it happen again this year."

Suddenly he opened his eyes and looked right at me. "Peter, I learned a lot in the last few weeks. I read more than you can imagine. I have millions of facts in my head that I'm trying to put together. I don't know what it all means, but I know the numbers. I know *one day's* worth of the money our world spends on guns and bombs and soldiers could save fifty million children over the next ten years."

As Duncan spoke I had a vision, a fantasy, that the people of Earth—not the leaders, not the government, just the people—were suddenly able to speak with one voice. And they said, "Enough. We don't want it to be this way anymore. *Make it right!*"

But we couldn't speak with one voice. For some reason we were no better than mute in the face of a disaster that we all wanted to pretend didn't exist.

I was sick with shame and anger. And I knew that I would never be the same after that night.

I had been witness to a crime.

Now I would have to testify to what I had seen. Because to keep silent would also be a crime.

CHAPTER NINE

Button Pushers

When that first flight was finally over we were all exhausted—and not just because we had stayed up for most of the night. It was the things we had seen, the feelings they had created, that were the most tiring. Even now I don't remember how I got out of the saucer and into bed. But I must have, somehow, because the next thing I knew the sun was shining in my face and I realized that I had a pillow beneath my head.

I wondered if Broxholm had carried me upstairs. I could remember my father doing that once, when I was very little.

I lay there for a while, staring at the ceiling and thinking about the night before. My mind kept coming back to the two doctors in Ethiopia, and the man who had died trying to save the boy on the battlefield in Asia. No one was forcing those doctors to stay there. No one had forced that man to risk his life for the boy.

Kreeblim had said we were looking for hope. We had found a little even in the worst of places. Maybe things weren't hope*less* after all.

After a while I noticed Big Julie's breathing. I glanced at the clock beside my bed. Almost noon. Fishing some clean clothes out of my backpack, I dressed and wandered downstairs.

Susan, Kreeblim, and Broxholm were in the kitchen already, eating breakfast. Since the aliens weren't wearing their masks, the scene looked like a cross between *Leave It to Beaver* and *The Twilight Zone*.

"Have a pleskit," said Kreeblim as I sat down. She handed me something round and purple.

I stared at it.

"You eat it," said Broxholm.

I had already figured that out. But I was thinking of the people we had seen the night before. How could I eat after that?

"Starving yourself won't help them," Broxholm said sharply, as if he had read my mind. *"Eat."*

I hesitated a bit longer, then took a bite, promising myself I would find some way to help change what we had seen.

The pleskit was thick, crusty, and delicious. Something inside it tasted like berries. I began to wonder if Kreeblim had chosen to disguise herself as a home economics teacher for a reason.

"So, what do we do now?" I asked as Duncan wandered into the room and Kreeblim handed him a pleskit.

"Fieldwork," replied Broxholm, tucking something brown and squirmy into his mouth.

"FOOD FIRST," rumbled Big Julie. "FIELD-WORK LATER."

Broxholm pulled on his nose. "I stand corrected. First we feed Big Julie. *Then* we start our fieldwork."

"Who gets to feed him?" asked Susan.

"YOU DO!"

Susan jumped a little. (Okay, I guess I did, too.)

"Don't worry," whispered Kreeblim, waving her nose. "He's just testing you. You can all do it together."

"How do we feed him?" asked Duncan nervously.

"That's his meal," said Broxholm, pointing to some buckets next to the sink. "He doesn't eat as much as you might expect."

"Well, not now," said Kreeblim, "but that's because he's fairly inactive at the moment."

"Anyway, finish your own meal first," said Broxholm. "Uhrbhighgjououol-lee can wait."

The floorboards rumbled with Big Julie's displeasure. I started to get to my feet, but Broxholm motioned for me to stay in my chair. "I said he can wait," he repeated softly.

"TRAITOR!"

"Not so," replied Broxholm, raising his voice only a little. "You know the codes as well as I do, Uhrbhighgjououol-lee."

Kreeblim's wormy lavender hair writhed in dismay. "Broxholm, there is no need to irritate him!"

"And there is no need for him to be discourteous to our friends," replied Broxholm, giving me a wink.

According to my translator, the wink meant nothing on Broxholm's native world. He was using it the same way we do, which was a little like speaking a foreign language with his body instead of his mouth.

My mind grabbed at the gesture. A wink. There was *something* about a wink that I ought to remember, or figure out.

What was it?

Puzzled, I smiled at Broxholm and returned my attention to my meal. I finished quickly, and as soon as Duncan and Susan were ready we crossed to the buckets, which were filled with a murky-looking concoction.

"What is this stuff?" I asked, turning my head to avoid the smell.

"Swamp water," Kreeblim replied.

"Local or imported?" asked Duncan.

Broxholm smiled. "Local. Big Julie likes to sample native cuisines."

I picked up a pair of buckets and headed down the hall. "I wonder what we're supposed to do next," said Susan, who was walking behind me. "I mean, you can't feed an eyeball, right?"

She shouldn't have worried. Big Julie had

shifted position. When I opened the door, I found myself face to face, so to speak, with the biggest mouth I had seen since Hoo-Lan took me for a ride in a Rhoomba.

If we hadn't been there to feed Big Julie, I might not have known it was a mouth. I didn't see any teeth; he didn't even have one of those gonger things hanging at the back of his throat. All I could see was a big black hole. The only real mouth clue was the foot-high ridge of brown and green flesh at the bottom of the door, which I think was his lower lip.

"Just toss the stuff in," called Broxholm from the kitchen.

"Peter, look out!" cried Duncan as I lifted my bucket. I jumped back barely in time to avoid a thick strip of moist brown and green flesh that rolled through the door and slapped into the opposite wall. It was textured like a sponge and covered with fist-sized knobs.

"*What* is that?" asked Susan.

"His tongue," said Duncan with a shudder.

"AHHHHHHHHHHH!"

I started to say, "Let's do this and get it over with," but held in the words for fear of insulting Big Julie. Not speaking, being careful to avoid stepping on the tongue, I got as close to the door as I could, then tossed in my buckets of swamp water. Susan did the same, and then Duncan. After a few seconds the great green and brown tongue slid back through the door. A wall of flesh descended over the black hole, and a sigh of contentment rumbled through the floorboards.

We closed the door and headed for the kitchen. As I was sitting down the cups on the table began to rattle, like you'd see in a film about an earthquake.

"Good," said Kreeblim, "he liked the meal."

The rumbling was Big Julie's belch of appreciation!

With Big Julie fed, we started to discuss our fieldwork again. To my surprise, the first thing the aliens wanted us to do was get disguises. That turned out to be more fun than I expected, partly because when it was time to make them, Kreeblim said, "Well, how would you like to look?" I didn't know how to respond at first. I had always wanted to look like the heroes on the covers of the science fiction books I read. But you couldn't put a face like that on a kid's body.

As it turned out, what I *could* do was use my URAT to design my mask. I sat and played with different features until I had a face I liked. Then I sent the design from my URAT to the mask machine. A few minutes later it delivered my new face.

Broxholm showed me how to put it on, then gave me a mirror. I stared at myself in astonishment; I had dark hair and eyes, a perfectly formed nose, and a mouth that somehow looked a lot

more heroic than mine. (I'm not sure exactly what makes a mouth look heroic, but believe me, mine did.)

I know you should judge people on the basis of what's inside, not how they look. Now I found I was judging *myself* by looks. With a different face, I *felt* different.

I wasn't entirely happy to discover this about myself.

"Maybe we should choose new names to go with our new faces," said Duncan, once we were all wearing our masks. "I want to be Albert."

Though he didn't say it, I was pretty sure he was naming himself after Albert Einstein. I didn't laugh, so it annoyed me when I said, "Okay. I'm going to be Stoney," and Duncan said, "Where did you get *that* name?"

I didn't want to say that Stoney was the name of my favorite science fiction hero. It took me a while to realize how funny it was that Duncan was naming himself after a great brain, while I was naming myself for an action hero.

"How about you, Susan?" asked Kreeblim.

"I'll just be Susan, thanks," she said with a smile. "I like my name just fine."

We spent the next two weeks traveling all over the world, looking at the best and the worst of what we humans do.

We roamed museums where I saw artwork so

beautiful it made me weep, and streets so thick with starving people that I woke up in the night, haunted by their hungry eyes.

We began to refer to the bad sights as button-pushers—things that might convince the aliens to use the red button.

Things that gave us hope—like the night we sat by a fire in Africa and listened to an old man tell a story of how the world began—were called button-busters. I was truly happy to have my Universal Translator that night. The storyteller's words pulled me into his spell, and I felt joined with all the other listeners, almost as if we were one being. It was one of the best nights of my life.

The next day we saw the worst button-pusher of all. That was the day we crept, invisible, into a prison where men and women were being tortured for disagreeing with their government. What had already been done to those people was so ugly I cannot bring myself to describe it, even though the memory of it remains like a scar burned into my brain with a hot iron.

Even worse was the moment when it was about to start again. When I saw what the uniformed man was going to do to the woman strapped to the table, I pressed myself against the wall and closed my eyes. But even with my hands clamped over my ears I couldn't shut out her scream.

The scream lasted less than half a second. For the first and only time during the entire mission, Broxholm broke the noninvolvement rule. When I opened my eyes, I saw that he had knocked the torturer unconscious.

I could spend pages telling you how we snuck the prisoners to freedom. It was quite an adventure, and Susan did an amazing thing. But it's not really part of this story. I'll tell you only that I still have nightmares about that room, and that Broxholm trembled with fury for an entire day afterwards. I think he was beginning to believe that maybe the red button was the only solution after all.

"To ignore the starving is one thing," he told me. "But to actively—" He broke off in a shudder.

"There is a great mystery here," said Kreeblim. "The best of what your people create shows a deep longing to join together. Yet the worst of what you do seems to come from some great separation, as if you don't even recognize yourselves as members of the same species."

"THEY'RE HOPELESS," said Big Julie.

They're hopeless. I wondered if that would be his message to the Interplanetary Council. I could hardly stand to bring him his swamp water that evening; it felt traitorous to be feeding a creature who believed we should be destroyed.

About ten minutes after Big Julie's wall-rattling burp of appreciation someone began knocking at the door.

Kreeblim was instantly alert, like a wild animal when it hears an unexpected sound. "Who could that be?" she whispered.

Indeed, no one should have been knocking at her door, since "Miss Karpou" was supposed to be out of town with Susan.

"Probably just some salesman," I whispered back.

The knocking sounded again, louder than before. "This is the police!" yelled a deep male voice. "Open up in there!"

"Plevvit!" said Kreeblim. This was a word from her own language, and it's so bad I have no translation for it.

More banging.

We had taken off our masks to relax, so neither Broxholm nor Kreeblim had on a human face. Susan was supposed to be away on her scholarship trip, and I was presumed to have been kidnapped by aliens; either of us answering the door would raise dangerous questions. That left Duncan, though if he were to go to the door the police would almost certainly insist on returning him to his home.

"Maybe we should just hide," said Susan.

BANG! BANG! BANG!

"No good," replied Broxholm. "It sounds like they're getting ready to break the door down. If they do that, they'll almost certainly find Big Julie."

He didn't have to explain what a disaster *that* would be.

"I'd better get it," said Duncan.

"Wait!" said Susan as he started toward the door.

"No," said Broxholm, "he's the only one who can do it. Come on—the rest of us have to get out of sight."

Glancing over my shoulder as we headed for the stairs, I wondered if Duncan would ever stop surprising me.

CHAPTER TEN

Evacuate!

I crouched on the stairway and listened as Duncan opened the door. Susan stood one step behind me, her hand on my shoulder.

"Holy Moses!" cried the man who had been demanding to be let in. "It's Duncan Dougal! We've been wondering where you were hiding. We got a call about an explosion in here. What have you been doing—blowing off dynamite?"

"He must mean Big Julie's burp!" whispered Susan, leaning close to my ear.

"I'm not doing anything," Duncan replied sullenly.

"Not doing anything but breaking into poor Miss Karpou's house while she's out of town," said a new voice. "Anyone else in there with you?"

"Yeah," sneered Duncan. "A bunch of aliens."

Susan tightened her grip on my shoulder. But I knew what Duncan was doing. He figured if he made the men angry, they might hustle him off without coming inside.

For a moment, it looked like his ploy would

work. "Come on, kid," said the second man, "we're taking you home."

Then the first man spoke again. "Better take a look inside, Andy—make sure the kid hasn't trashed the place."

Susan and I began backing up the stairs as Andy came through the door. Suddenly, I realized something was different about the house. I couldn't figure out what it was—until I realized I couldn't hear Big Julie breathing. Wondering if he was holding his breath, I took another step backwards and almost screamed when I bumped into Broxholm, who was crouched at the top of the stairs. Broxholm put a finger to his lips, then lifted me to the top of the stairs. Turning around, he picked up Susan and set her next to me.

I could hear Andy walking around below us. Suddenly he shouted, "Yetch! What is this?"

I wondered what he had found until I glanced at Kreeblim. The worried writhing of her hair told me the problem: her poot was still on the kitchen table!

I hoped the thing had enough sense to stay in its blob form. That way it would just look like a gob of disgusting goo. If it lifted its head and went "Poot!", Andy might really freak out.

I waited to hear a scream. Nothing. After a moment, Andy's footsteps started down the hall. Was he going to open all of the doors? If so, he was in for a big surprise when he got to Big Julie's room!

I glanced behind me. Kreeblim was pulling on a mask, a non—Betty Lou Karpou face. I figured she was going to try to divert Andy's investigation. But before she could move, Duncan screamed, "Let go of me, you big brute!"

"Hey!" bellowed the cop. "Hey, watch it kid! *Owwww!*"

I smiled to myself. Duncan's life as a jerk hadn't been entirely wasted. He had just kicked the guy holding him in the shins in order to draw Andy's attention away from the house.

I blinked and shook my head. *How did I know what Duncan had just done—and why he had done it?*

A familiar wave of dizziness passed through me. Before I could even think of fainting, we heard a scream.

"Ahhhhhhhh!" cried Andy, sounding a lot like Duncan had the day he accidentally turned on the communication device that went to the alien spaceship. *"Ahhhhhhhhhh!"*

His scream was interrupted by a rush of wind as Big Julie let out his breath.

I think the thudding sound that followed was Andy getting blown against a wall. A swamplike stench filled the house. Next came the sound of someone throwing up, then running footsteps as Andy raced along the hall. "We've got to get out

of here!" he screamed as he burst through the front door.

"Why?" asked the other guy. "What's going on?"

"Don't ask! Don't talk! Just get out of here!"

"Lemme go!" yelled Duncan. "Hey, lemme go! I don't want to get in that car with you guys!"

The men ignored his complaints. Seconds later we heard the car start, then race away.

"Plevvit!" said Kreeblim.

"What do we do now?" asked Susan.

"Evacuate!" said Broxholm. "Everything that might provide even a hint that we have been here has to go."

"STARTING WITH ME," rumbled Big Julie.

"Yes, starting with you!" shouted Broxholm.

The next half-hour was a blur as we rushed to load the aliens' equipment into Kreeblim's saucer. Susan and I took turns watching at the front windows for any sign of the police. It was hard to tell when they might return; it depended on how scared they were, and what kind of weapons and how much manpower they decided to gather.

If we had been living in a cheap horror movie, they would have been back soon, with just a few men and some guns. But Kennituck Falls had already had one experience with aliens. They were not apt to take this lightly.

I saw something slouching down the hall behind me. I turned to get a better look, and turned back with a shudder when I realized it was a *piece* of Big Julie, heading for the transport beam that would take it back to the *New Jersey*.

I wondered what we would be doing next. Would we establish another base of operations— or would the mission be canceled altogether? If that happened, what would the alien council decide to do about Earth?

A car pulled up outside. It didn't park right in front of the house, but stopped where the driver would have a clear view of the place. A minute later another car pulled up.

"We're being watched," I said.

Kreeblim joined me at the window. "Plevvit," she whispered.

"One more load," said Broxholm. "Peter, Susan, grab those components. Let's see if we can do this in one trip."

Terrified that the police would break in before we could make our escape, I picked up the things Broxholm had pointed to and headed for the secret cellar. Susan was right behind me.

"Peter," she said, "this is really going to mess things up. We've got to do something."

That was Susan; ten thousand planets trying to figure out what to do about Earth, and she feels it's her personal responsibility to deal with the situation.

"Any suggestions?" I asked.

"Not yet," said Susan.

Soon Kreeblim joined us in the secret cellar. We finished loading the saucer while Broxholm used a pencil-sized laser beam to seal the door so no one could enter the space we were about to leave.

As soon as we were all in our places on the saucer, Kreeblim set the controls. We rolled forward. The backyard lifted. We shot into the air.

As we did, we heard a roar beneath us.

The police were shooting at the house!

I knew they were afraid; I was afraid, too. But I didn't think this would be taken as a good sign by the Interplanetary Council.

Well, that was the least of our problems at the moment.

"What are we going to do about Duncan?" I asked as we soared into the sky.

Kreeblim's hair waved in distress. "I don't know. If he talks about what we're doing, it could cause a great disruption. If things get too messy, the council may simply call off the mission."

"And if that happens?" Susan asked.

"Let's just say that we'd better find Duncan," said Broxholm.

His words gave me a shiver. I looked at the world below, and thought about The Button.

The end of the planet seemed to be getting closer by the minute.

CHAPTER ELEVEN

Duncan, Duncan, Who's Got the Duncan?

Unfortunately, going after Duncan was complicated by the fact that rumors about Andy seeing a giant alien in Miss Karpou's house began to spread at rocket speed. The result was that the entire town of Kennituck Falls started to go berserk.

In any other town such rumors might have been laughed off. But people in Kennituck Falls *knew* that aliens existed; a lot of them had seen Broxholm unmasked at our school concert the previous spring. My going off with him had only made things worse, since most grownups couldn't accept the idea that I had *chosen* to go, and so had convinced themselves that he had kidnapped me. Now they were worried that more children might be "abducted."

We learned about the rumors through the equipment in Kreeblim's saucer, which could pick up anything the police sent over their radios. We set it to record broadcasts from all over the state. The computer then scanned the broadcasts for key words like *Duncan*, *alien*, and *invasion*. Within hours we learned that people were locking their kids inside, buying guns, and stocking up on ammunition.

I thought the panic was in full swing.

Actually, it was just getting started.

We also learned that while the police search had not yet found anything unusual in Miss Karpou's house, they were seriously considering digging up the backyard.

Broxholm ground his purple teeth at that news. "If they dig, they'll find proof we were there. Then they'll bring in the federal government, maybe even the military."

"Will there be a war?" I asked, remembering what the aliens had said about their projections.

"No telling," he replied, stretching his nose further than I had ever seen it go before.

To make things worse, the rumors convinced the Simmonses that Susan was being held prisoner by aliens. We learned about this when our news scans picked up an interview with the Simmonses. They were hysterical.

"Susan Simmons, phone home!" I said.

"Excellent idea," said Kreeblim, as she began manipulating the control panel. "A call from Susan right now could do much to settle their nerves."

The next thing I knew, Susan's father said, "Greetings!"

It took me a moment to realize that Kreeblim had somehow dialed Susan's home and reached the family answering machine. The message from Susan's father ended. The machine beeped.

"Go ahead," Kreeblim whispered, nodding at Susan. *"Talk!"*

Susan nodded back, then said, "Mom—Dad? Hi, it's me! Just wanted to let you know that everything is going great. Kree—er—Miss Karpou and I are having a super time. I'm learning more than I ever expected to."

Boy, did she say that line with feeling!

"Well, sorry I missed you. I don't have the phone number for where we're going to be next, so I'll call again tomorrow. Hope everything is all right!"

She nodded, and Kreeblim cut the connection.

"I hope that makes them feel better," said Susan.

"I suspect it will," said Broxholm. "Which means our biggest worry now is retrieving Duncan."

"I'll be able to locate him with no problem," said Kreeblim. "He was carrying the transmitter we gave him in Africa, and I can get a fix on that. But knowing where he is won't tell us who has him, or how they're treating him."

"My guess is that the government will take

custody of him," said Broxholm. "Or at least send someone to keep an eye on him."

"They won't get much out of him if he doesn't want them to," I said. "Duncan's an incredible liar." I stopped, then added, "Well, I know he's different now that he's so much smarter, but brains don't have anything to do with lying. It's not like being smart makes you honest or anything." That still didn't sound very good, so I just said, "What I mean is, he's had a lot of practice." Then I shut up.

"It's all right that you don't like Duncan," said Broxholm. "You don't have to hide it from us, as if we would use it as evidence against the planet. Not every being in the galaxy gets along with every other being. I deal with many beings I can barely tolerate."

"Then why are you so upset about *us?*" asked Susan.

"Because we don't think disliking a being, disagreeing with it, or even getting furious with it is sufficient reason to kill it."

"But that's exactly what you're talking about doing to our whole planet!" said Susan angrily.

Broxholm tugged on his nose. "It's what *some* of us are advocating. And while I disagree with the idea, I can tell you at least two things that make it different. First, your species has a habit of killing; you do it all the time. We have never done anything like this before. Second, if we *do* do this, it will be for the sole purpose of trying to prevent a greater tragedy." He paused. "Perhaps that is the real difference. We *will* see it as a tragedy. You may not have understood that from what you have heard so far. But I tell you truly, if we decide to end human life, we will not rejoice, nor brag in song of our conquests and all we have killed. There will be no victory celebration, but a time of sorrow. Indeed, we shall mourn as we have never mourned before, because such a thing was found to be necessary."

If that was supposed to make me feel better, it didn't work.

"So what do we do about Duncan?" I asked.

"I think we should try to get him back right away," said Broxholm. "He may be good at lying, but I don't know how long he'll be able to resist the techniques they may try on him."

"What do you mean, techniques?" asked Susan.

"Your government has ways of making people talk," said Kreeblim. "Not all of them are pleasant."

Susan's eyes grew wide. "But Duncan is just a kid!"

Kreeblim's purple hair leaned to the right. "Child though Duncan may be, if agents of your government feel the danger is sufficient, they will not hesitate to do whatever they convince themselves is necessary."

I figured Kreeblim was just guessing at this—until I remembered Broxholm's previous words about monitoring secret government transmissions. Then I shivered.

"However, I doubt it will come to that," Kreeblim continued. "More likely Duncan will simply tell them what they want to know."

Susan shook her head. "He's changed, but he's still Duncan—which means, among other things, that he's incredibly stubborn. He won't forget that you said if word of this got out, you might have to end the mission, that it could even cause a war. If Duncan believes the safety of the world depends on him keeping his mouth shut, he might try to tough out anything they do to him."

"I think we should go after him," said Broxholm.

"This is the kind of thing Big Julie is supposed to be watching for," said Kreeblim uncomfortably. "Us getting too involved with the natives."

I frowned. "Big Julie's not here."

"He'll be back," replied Kreeblim.

"Then we'd better hurry, hadn't we?" asked Susan, her eyes flashing with anger.

"Child!" said Kreeblim. "Do you understand that the failure of this mission could lead to the end of your species?"

"I understand it, and I think it stinks!" Susan snapped. "But there's not much I can do about that. You either, I guess. Personally, I think you're a bunch of loons, but there's not much I can do about that, either. What we can do is get Duncan, since he got into this by trying to shield us."

Broxholm looked at Kreeblim. He pulled his nose and let it snap back into place.

Hair squirming, Kreeblim nodded and said, "We'd best start by figuring out where he is." Turning to the control panel, she touched several of the spheres. After a moment, her nose began to twitch in agitation. Soon it began to slap against her cheek.

"What's the matter?" asked Broxholm.

Kreeblim's wormy hair was writhing in dismay now. Her voice filled with astonishment, she said, "I can't locate him."

"What do you mean?" asked Susan.

Kreeblim returned her attention to the panel and began frantically manipulating control devices. Without looking at us, she said desperately, "Duncan has disappeared!"

"That doesn't make any sense," said Broxholm. "He's got to be *somewhere*."

"Do *you* want to work the controls?" asked Kreeblim, her nose slapping even more sharply against her cheek.

For a moment I thought they were going to have a fight, which was the last thing we really needed. But Broxholm simply said, "No, I trust you."

"I don't understand," said Susan. "Even if something happened to Duncan, shouldn't you be able to locate the transmitter?"

"Of course," said Kreeblim. "That's what makes this so disturbing. That transmitter is very powerful, and nearly indestructible. Even if it was taken from him and put at the bottom of a mineshaft, my sensors should be able to detect it."

"Wait!" said Broxholm. "The monitors have picked up something."

Silence fell in the cabin as the computer played back a police broadcast.

"Duncan Dougal has disappeared from custody," said a deep voice. "Begin an intensive search for this boy; national security issues may be at stake."

"What the heck is going on?" asked Susan, her eyes wide.

"I don't know," replied Broxholm. His nose was twitching with anxiety. "I truly don't know."

CHAPTER TWELVE

The Final Days

We spent the rest of that long night circling Kennituck Falls, trying to locate Duncan. We had no success. At last, reluctantly, the aliens decided we should return to our task, starting by preparing a new headquarters.

"Perhaps we should use the farm," suggested Kreeblim.

"Probably the best idea," agreed Broxholm. "It's the most isolated of our places."

"Your *places*?" asked Susan.

Kreeblim closed her middle eye. "We bought several pieces of property last year."

Susan nudged me. "If the people who are upset about the Japanese buying American buildings get word of this one, they're really going to wig out!" she whispered.

The farm was about ten miles from Kennituck Falls, and it was great—fifty acres of quiet countryside, with a big old house that was filled with nooks and crannies. It took us about half a day to get ready to move in. Most of that time went to creating a hiding place for the saucer, this time not beneath the house, but under the nearby barn.

Once the hangar was ready Broxholm and I used power tools from the saucer to dig a tunnel to the basement of the house. To my surprise I enjoyed doing the work. It was good to do something real, and I liked working side by side with Broxholm.

After we finished the tunnel, Big Julie returned from the *New Jersey*, one piece at a time.

"I CANNOT SAY IT IS GOOD TO BE BACK," he rumbled after reassembling himself in his new room. "BUT IT CERTAINLY IS INTERESTING. THINGS ARE LOOKING BAD. HOW ABOUT LUNCH?"

Since Susan was busy with something else, I carried eight buckets of swamp water to his door by myself.

"THANK YOU SO MUCH," he said when I was done. "IS IT SAFE TO DIGEST?"

"According to Broxholm, that's one reason we're on this farm—so you can burp without disturbing the neighbors."

"GOOD," said Big Julie, just before he set the walls to shaking.

As I was walking away he said, "BY THE WAY—I TALKED THE COUNCIL OUT OF CANCELING THE MISSION AFTER DUNCAN DISAPPEARED."

I turned back and looked at his door. "Why?"

I asked, which may have been a little rude, but was an indication of how astonished I was.

"THIS IS TOO INTERESTING TO END RIGHT NOW," he said. Then, after a long pause, he added, "BESIDES, I LIKE YOU."

He sounded embarrassed. I felt like I should say, "I like you, too." Only I figured he would know that was a lie, so I just said, "Thank you. Very much."

"DON'T MENTION IT," he replied. "*EVER!*"

I had a feeling he was serious.

"You have my word," I said.

The next morning, still fretting about Duncan, we started our research again. We had only a few days left before it would be time to return and make our report, and about the only hope we were finding was the fact that no matter where we went, no matter how bad things were, there were always a few people trying to make things better.

Memory: walking along a city street lined with homeless people sleeping on the sidewalks. I saw a man who lived in a cardboard box reading a paperback book on philosophy.

Memory: standing in a welfare hotel where the government was paying two thousand dollars a month to keep a family of five in a single room. My father had told me how much he paid each month for our house. As I watched the mother flick roaches from the baby's bed, I tried to figure out why the government would pay three times that amount to keep people in a place like this. A rat ran across my feet, and under the bed.

Memory: spending a day in a school that was so crowded some kids had to have classes in the bathroom because there was no place else to put them. We went to another school where the kids couldn't use the playground, because it was contaminated with toxic waste.

In case you're wondering, that was all here, right in this country. Not that things were much better in other places. But it always seemed weirder to me when we saw it here, because our country is so rich.

"It's amazing," agreed Kreeblim as her hair writhed in confusion. "Your impulses are so good, and yet the problems go on. I don't understand it at all."

"BAD BLOOD," said Big Julie. "SOMETHING SICK INSIDE."

I hated it when he said things like that, partly because I didn't know how to argue with him. We all knew by now that the problems weren't universal; we had seen too many good things to believe that. But we also knew that the fact that humans did *some* good things wasn't going to be enough to convince the aliens it was safe to let us out into the galaxy—not as long as they saw the *rest* of the things we were doing.

What I was really worried about was whether it would be enough to convince them to let us survive.

Sometimes after Broxholm and Kreeblim had gone to their own rooms, Susan and I would build a fire in the big wood-burning stove in the farmhouse kitchen. Then we would sit and talk. We knew Big Julie could hear us, but after a while we got used to that, and didn't let it stop us— partly because we felt we *had* to talk, both to work through the things that we were seeing, and to try to find some way to make sense of it all.

Broxholm and Kreeblim didn't seem to care how late the two of us stayed up. "Just make sure you get enough sleep," Kreeblim said one morning, after Susan and I had been talking long into the night.

Usually Susan talked to her parents first. To convince the Simmonses that Susan was still traveling with Miss Karpou, the aliens set up a system where Susan could give her parents different long distance numbers that, when dialed, would get bounced to where we were staying.

Mr. and Mrs. Simmons often talked about the alien scare, and said that they were glad Susan was safely out of town.

"I miss my parents," Susan confessed to me one night, after one of these conversations.

At least you've got parents to miss, I thought.

But I didn't say that, because I didn't want to get into a game of "Who's the most miserable."

"Are you worried about them?" I asked.

"I'm worried about *everyone*," said Susan bleakly. "I keep thinking about what will happen if the aliens choose Plan D. I have dreams about that button."

"Me too," I admitted.

As the end of the mission drew closer, the dreams got worse. Also Susan and I noticed something strange: even as we were seeing the planet at its worst, we were both falling more and more in love with it.

"I just want to fix things," she said to me one night. "I want to make it better."

Of course, she had always been that way. But now she had an even clearer idea of how much needed fixing!

The other thing that happened every night was that Kreeblim spent time trying to locate Duncan. "I simply cannot understand it," she said nervously. "What could have happened to him?"

But for that we had no answer. Sometimes after I had gone to bed I would stare at the ceiling and try to make telepathic contact with him. A couple of times I almost thought I had something. But then I would get dizzy, and it would fade away.

Though the alien scare was pretty much confined to our state, it continued to get worse. For some reason a lot of people had decided that the aliens were ready to invade and that the government was trying to keep things quiet.

The more the rumors spread, the more the fear grew. The week after Andy had seen Big Julie, a small group from Kennituck Falls staged an anti-alien demonstration in the state capital. And two days before we were scheduled to return to the *New Jersey* our monitors picked up a police report that roving gangs of teenagers were attacking and beating people they accused of being aliens.

"See how you fear the other, the outsider?" asked Broxholm the next morning. "This is the source of many problems."

"But there must be a reason for it," said Kreeblim. "There must be some root cause for so much fear and hatred. If we could discover that root, maybe we could find a cure."

It was the most hopeful thing that I had heard either of them say in a couple of weeks.

"Perhaps we should go to one of these demonstrations," said Broxholm. "Maybe we'll learn something from it."

I wasn't sure about this. I figured people would be saying—shouting—things that might really offend the aliens. When I mentioned that, Kreeblim replied, "What can we hear that is more offensive than what we have already seen? We have to return to the ship tomorrow. We may as well do this today."

Tomorrow? I felt a clutch of fear. Tomorrow we would go back to space. Tomorrow, we would report to the Interplanetary Council.

Tomorrow, the fate of the Earth would be decided.

Which made it oddly fitting, I suppose, that later that afternoon I found myself in a march around the capitol, carrying a sign that demanded ACTION AGAINST THE ALIENS.

I had never been in a demonstration before. I was amazed at how energy seemed to flow through the group. As the emotions grew stronger a kind of electricity seemed to bind the crowd together. To my astonishment, I felt myself being sucked into the group, as if I had become a part of something larger than myself.

The shouting grew louder, the chants more ferocious. People made speeches claiming that the government was hiding the truth about "the alien menace."

Then someone threw a rock.

That was all it took for the situation to erupt.

Before I knew it the crowd had become a mob. Soon the police were shooting tear gas. Within minutes, the demonstration turned into a riot.

As the first bit of gas began to burn at my eyes and nose the crowd was flowing like a living thing, splitting into pieces, then reforming. It made me think of Big Julie.

As the mob surged back and forth across the

open square in front of the capitol I was actually picked up and carried by the momentum of the crowd. Soon I had lost track of Broxholm, Kreeblim, and Susan. A moment later I fell. For a few terrifying seconds people were trampling over me. Then a man and a woman stopped to help me to my feet, even though that put them in danger of being run over themselves.

Coughing, gasping, choking, I worked my way to the edge of the square where a little girl grabbed me by the arm.

"Krepta!" she cried, dragging me toward an alley, "Thank goodness I found you."

I had been chased, stepped on, and gassed. At the moment I was too dazed to wonder why this kid was calling me by my alien name. I just followed her.

CHAPTER THIRTEEN

Sharleen

I stood in the alley, gasping for breath, and looked at the kid who had dragged me from the riot. She was shorter than me, dressed in ragged clothes. She had shaggy brown hair and big eyes. She was fairly ugly, as kids go.

"Why did you do bring me here?" I asked when my breathing had slowed a bit. Suddenly I realized what she had said when she first saw me. "And why did you call me Krepta? Who are you, anyway?"

She smiled. "People around here call me Sharleen. But you know me by another name."

I stared at her. After a moment, she put her fingers to her neck and pulled aside just enough skin to reveal a patch of blue underneath.

"Hoo-Lan!" I cried with joy.

"You were expecting maybe Darth Vader?"

"Where have you been? How long have you been better? Why didn't you join us? Have you been—"

"Peace, peace!" he said, putting up his hands to stop my flow of questions. "One at a time.

I've been working in my own way, which is what I usually do. You have to understand, Peter, that I am a bit of a renegade. The Interplanetary Council does not entirely approve of me." He paused, then said, "Actually, I don't think they approve of me at all. But they feel they owe me some respect, since I used to be Prime Member."

I looked at him in awe. "*Prime Member?* Does that mean what I think it does?"

Hoo-Lan smiled. "If you mean was I ruler of the galaxy, the answer is yes."

"I knew it! You kept putting me off when I asked who you really were. But I knew there was something special about you."

"There's something special about everyone," said Hoo-Lan. Then he waved his hand in a very earthlinglike gesture. "Anyway, don't take that Prime Member thing too seriously. Title aside, I didn't have as much power as you might think. That was one reason I resigned; it was too hard to get things done. To tell you the truth, there were times when I had to resort to being downright sneaky."

I wanted to ask him when and why, but he waved his hand again. "Enough of that! I want to know how things have gone with your mission."

"Not very well," I said, feeling a sudden depression at admitting the fact. "We've found a lot of stuff, both good and bad, but I don't think anything we've found will convince the council to let us into the Interplanetary League."

Of course, that wasn't the real issue.

"I'm not sure anything will convince them it's safe to let us continue to exist."

Hoo-Lan nodded.

"How are things out there?" I asked, rolling my eyes skyward.

"Not good. Opinion is shifting against you—especially since we're doing a close monitoring now, and the anti-alien demonstrations are being reported across the galaxy."

"That's not fair! The main reason those demonstrations are going on is that you guys have scared people."

"I would think the idea that you are not alone in the universe would make you feel *safer*," said Hoo-Lan. "The reaction on every other planet at finding other life in the galaxy has been joy. They rejoice because it doesn't occur to them to be afraid. You fear because it doesn't occur to you to rejoice. Which is a large part of the problem."

I wasn't in the mood for another lecture on the moral flaws of earthlings. "Did you hear about Duncan?" I asked.

Hoo-Lan smiled. "I not only heard about Duncan, I tended to the situation."

"What do you—"

The end of my question was drowned out by a

roar from the end of the alley. The riot seemed to be getting worse.

"Come on!" said Hoo-Lan, taking my arm. "We have to get out of here. We can talk more later."

"I can't leave without Susan and the others!"

Hoo-Lan dragged me to the end of the alley. The crowd still surged back and forth. A whiff of tear gas made my eyes sting. "Do you think you can find them out there?" he asked.

I shook my head. It was impossible.

"What do we do?" I asked.

"Can you go invisible?"

I nodded.

"Then best do so. If we keep our backs to the buildings and our hands in contact, we should be able to get into the open. We'll decide what to do next after we're in the clear."

I switched myself invisible and followed him. Side by side, hands touching, we eased our way along the edge of the mob. I felt again how it was like a living thing, with the people seeming to act as a single mass rather than as individuals.

Several people were pushed so close they touched me. Normally, brushing against an invisible person would have caused them to draw away in fear. Now, with their focus on the riot, they barely noticed.

Where were Susan, Broxholm, and Kreeblim? I hoped they had managed to get out safely. I remembered how it had felt when I fell and people were running over me, and shuddered at the idea of that happening to Susan.

It took nearly fifteen minutes to get away from the riot. Once we were clear of it we ran for several blocks before stopping to become visible again.

"What an experience!" I gasped, leaning against a wall.

"Remember it!" said Hoo-Lan. "It may be part of the answer."

"What do you mean? If your people saw that, they'd probably decide to get rid of us immediately."

Hoo-Lan shrugged. I had noticed that of all the aliens, he was the one whose gestures were most humanlike. Another alien's shrugs or winks might mean anything from "You have beautiful ear hair" to "Run away!" But with Hoo-Lan, such gestures rarely needed translation.

"CrocDoc is still analyzing the data he gathered when he removed your brain," he said. "He has a whole team of scientists working on it. They're also examining what happened to me when I made contact with your brain."

"I'm sorry about that. I didn't mean to hurt you."

"Of course you didn't! Anyway, it was my fault for moving too fast. Scary experience, though; I certainly wasn't prepared for the vastness of what

I found. We can talk about that once things settle down. For now, we have to figure out where to go next."

"Shouldn't we go back to our base of operations?"

He shrugged again. "It depends on what we want to do. It might be interesting for Broxholm and Kreeblim if you go missing, too. Give them a bit to think about."

"They'll be terrified!"

"A little terror won't hurt them. It may loosen up their juices, get them thinking more clearly."

Whatever had happened to Hoo-Lan while he was in his coma, he had come out of it as strange and confusing as ever.

"Where do *you* think we should go?" I asked.

"I've been staying at a shelter for kids on the run. You're a little young for it, but I think you'll be all right there. Might do you some good. You'll meet a few old friends."

"Old friends?"

Hoo-Lan smiled mysteriously. I knew him well enough to know that I wasn't likely to get any more information out of him at this point. With a sigh, I started to follow him. We must have walked for a mile or two, ending up in a section of the city that I would have been happier to visit with Broxholm at my side, since he's the strongest being I have ever met. Coming here with Hoo-Lan didn't feel nearly so safe, especially since it was starting to get dark.

"Here we are!" he said as we reached a building that looked like it had once been a church. A wooden sign in front announced that it was the Tisha Hamilton Home for Wayward Boys. Only *Boys* had been crossed out and the word *Youth* painted above it, so I assumed they had decided not to discriminate on the basis of sex.

"You'd better call me Sharleen as long as we're in here," said Hoo-Lan as he opened the door.

I felt pretty nervous when we stepped inside; most of the kids hanging around looked older and tougher than me. Then "Sharleen" led me to a kid sitting against the wall and whispered, "Peter, this is someone you know quite well."

The kid stood up.

"Peter?"

My eyes went wide.

"Duncan?"

"Shhh! In this place I'm known as Roger."

Duncan was wearing a mask that made his face look completely different. I was beginning to feel like no one had his or her own face anymore.

Then I saw two people who *did* have their own faces, a man and a woman leading a discussion group in the far corner of the main room. The shock was so powerful that my knees began to wobble and I had to grab Hoo-Lan's arm to keep from collapsing.

CHAPTER FOURTEEN

Jealousy

I took a moment to recover, then stepped closer.

The woman leading the discussion group looked very familiar. She should have; I had spent the better part of a year in her classroom. It was Ms. Marie Schwartz, our sixth-grade teacher—the one Broxholm had locked in a force field in his attic.

The man was even more familiar; he was my father.

"What's *he* doing here?" I whispered.

"Why not ask him and find out?" replied Hoo-Lan quietly.

That made me angry. "If you want me to start asking direct questions, let's begin with you. Why did you bring *me* here?"

Hoo-Lan shrugged. "I thought you might learn something."

"Maybe I don't want to learn this!" I hissed.

He shrugged again and said, "I'm your teacher."

"I'd rather have a math lesson."

"Not your choice."

Duncan leaned toward me. "They're dating," he whispered.

"*What!*"

Everyone turned to look at us. I started to blush, though I'm not sure whether that actually showed through my mask. Duncan gestured to the group that everything was all right. They returned to their discussion.

"Your father is going out with Ms. Schwartz," he whispered.

I didn't answer; I couldn't think of anything to say.

"Come on, let's go to my room," said Duncan after a few moments of silence.

I nodded, since that made as much sense as anything at the moment.

Duncan led us into a shabby corridor that had many doors opening off either side. The fifth door on the left opened into a room with three bunk beds and three battered-looking dressers. Duncan climbed onto one of the top bunks. "Come on up," he said, motioning to Hoo-Lan and me. We climbed the ladder and joined him. "Remember to go invisible if anyone comes in," Duncan said to Hoo-Lan as we were settling in.

"Of course!"

"Girls aren't supposed to hang out in the boys' rooms," Duncan explained to me as Hoo-Lan fluffed a pillow.

I had so many questions bouncing around in my brain that I didn't know where to start. Finally I decided to try for the beginning. "When did you come out of your coma?" I asked Hoo-Lan.

"Shortly before you left the ship. Remember when you fainted in the council chamber?"

"How could I forget it?"

"Well, what caused it was our minds brushing as I started to come around. I was still fairly groggy; delirious, actually. But I knew I was going to be all right—though I didn't want the council to know it yet. That's why I gave you that signal when you came to visit me, so you wouldn't have to worry about me."

"Signal?"

Hoo-Lan looked surprised. "Didn't you understand?"

Before he could finish I slapped my forehead as something that had been nagging at the back of my mind for weeks suddenly became clear. "You winked at me!" I cried, remembering how he had slowly opened and closed one eye when I was standing in his room on the *New Jersey*.

My pleasure at figuring that out was modified by another question. "So has this all been just a big joke to you?" I asked, trying to decide whether I was angry.

"Jokes can be very serious," said Hoo-Lan, sounding dead serious himself. "On the other hand, most serious things are terribly funny when you look at them from the right angle."

"Could we skip the philosophy and go straight to the information?"

He shrugged. "I was playing possum, to use an Earth phrase. Reasons? Number one: I did not want to be included in your mission. Number two: I did not want my enemies to know I was still in the game. Later, when I was more fully recovered, I 'woke up' long enough to cause some excitement. This gave me a chance to ask a friend to help me with a bit of a deception. I appeared to drift in and out of my coma several times over the next few days, which gave me a chance to make a switch." He smiled. "There is still *something* in that bubble back in the ship. And it is pretty comatose. Fortunately, it only looks like me."

I frowned. "Wouldn't technology as sophisticated as what you have on the *New Jersey* immediately detect that you had put something in your place?"

"As technology advances the technology to fool it advances, too. There's a nice balance in that, don't you think?"

I nodded, thinking many other things as well. "So when did you come down here?"

"When I heard that Duncan had been taken captive by your police force."

To my surprise, I felt jealous. Hoo-Lan was *my*

teacher, and I didn't like the idea that he had spent this time with Duncan.

"Why didn't you join us?" I asked.

"I was still not ready to let it be known that I was up and about," said Hoo-Lan. "I certainly didn't want to have to work out every step of what I did with Kreeblim and Broxholm. Even less did I want Uhrbhighgjououol-lee breathing down my neck. The two of us have never gotten along very well."

"What did you want to do that you couldn't do in front of them?"

"I've been doing telepathy experiments with Duncan."

"Are you trying to kill yourself?" I cried.

What I didn't ask, partly because I was afraid of the answer, was whether he had made contact with Duncan's brain and survived. I still feared there was something about *my* brain in particular that had driven him into his coma.

"Peace!" said Hoo-Lan, holding up his hands. "I didn't take any unnecessary chances. It wasn't easy, but I restrained myself. No machines this time."

Duncan spoke up. "As part of the experiments, Hoo-Lan has been helping me learn how to use my brain—teaching me ways to focus my mind and clear my thoughts. That was a relief, since it's so powerful right now it was driving me crazy." He smiled, a brave, sad smile. "I think I may be able to cope all right when the brain-fry starts to fade."

"That's good," I said, realizing that Duncan really did seem different, more calm somehow.

"Oh, I know what I wanted to ask you!" he said. "Would you like a poot?"

"What?"

"Do you want a poot? I can make you one. It turns out they don't mind being split. You just have to give them plenty of salt and water and let them rest for a bit afterwards. I've been making new ones for the kids in the shelter."

"You're kidding!" I cried. Turning to Hoo-Lan, I asked, "Won't that cause all kinds of problems?"

"Possibly," said Hoo-Lan. "Maybe it was a bad idea."

Duncan shrugged. "I did ask the other kids to keep them a secret."

I couldn't believe how calmly the two of them were taking this. I was sure Kreeblim wouldn't take it that way. In fact, I had a feeling she would be furious.

"How did you end up in this place?" I asked.

"I wanted to observe your old teacher for a while," replied Hoo-Lan. "I checked around and learned she was working here. So we came here, too. Finding your father was an unexpected bonus."

"In your opinion!"

"As you will," said Hoo-Lan calmly. Duncan went to one of the dressers and pulled out a plastic container. Inside was his poot. I wondered how many copies of the thing he had passed out already. Then I wondered if the kids he had given them to were splitting their poots as well.

"How long do they have to rest between—uh—splittings?"

"About half a day, if you don't keep them in the refrigerator like Kreeblim did," said Duncan.

Half a day! I did a little mental arithmetic. Divide a poot at noon, and you have two poots. Divide both of those at midnight and you have four. If you split them all again at noon *and* midnight the next day, you're up to sixteen. At the end of the next day you would have sixty-four. At the end of the fifth day you would have over a thousand poots. In less than ten days you could have more than a hundred thousand of the things!

I looked around nervously, half expecting to see poots hanging from the ceiling, climbing out of the dressers, oozing under the door.

"Poots are very important," said Hoo-Lan happily.

"Poot!" said the poot as Duncan squeezed it.

I blacked out and fell off the bed.

CHAPTER FIFTEEN

Connections

I woke to find a pair of unfamiliar faces in front of me and a painful head bump behind me.

After a second, I realized that the strangers staring down at me were Duncan and Hoo-Lan, still in their Roger and Sharleen masks.

I was getting a little sick of everyone going around wearing faces that weren't their own. I wanted to rip off my own mask, which suddenly felt suffocating. But then my father or Ms. Schwartz might see me, and who could tell what kind of trouble that might create?

"I knew there was a connection!" said Hoo-Lan joyfully.

"What is that supposed to mean?" I asked as Duncan helped me to my feet.

"People, poots, and telepathy," said Hoo-Lan. "You and Duncan have been telepathically linked before, with the help of machines. I don't think we need machines. I want to get past that, and the poots seem to help somehow. I think they're like an antenna for your brain."

"Probably I'd better not squeeze this one anymore," said Duncan, looking at his poot doubt-fully. "It seems to have a very close connection with Peter."

"That may have to do with the times that you two have been mentally connected through ma-chines," said Hoo-Lan. "We've got psychic wires crossing here that I can't understand yet."

"Wonderful," I said. "How about we all link minds and face the end of the world together?"

"Don't be so gloomy," said Hoo-Lan. "If you're all right, why don't you call the others and ask them to come get you?"

That was fine with me. Settling down on the lower bunk, I took my URAT from my pocket and tried to contact Broxholm or Kreeblim. I got no answer, which worried me. I hoped nothing had happened to them.

"I'll try again in a few minutes," I said, "every five minutes until I reach them."

"In the meantime, I'll show you around," said Duncan. "It's a strange place, but I kind of like it."

"Okay," I said. "Give me a tour. You coming—*Sharleen*?"

Hoo-Lan shook his head. "I have work to do. I'll see you later."

I'm sure you will, I thought. Out loud, I said, "Fine. See you soon."

"Why are you two staying here?" I asked Dun-can as we started down the hall. I thought I might get a different answer out of him once we were away from Hoo-Lan.

But he pretty much stuck to the same line. "Hoo-Lan didn't want to join up with you guys yet, for whatever reason. It's hard to know what he's planning from one minute to the next."

"I've noticed!"

"Anyway, we could have stayed in a hotel, but he said he would learn more by being here. I'm sure he chose the place because Ms. Schwartz works here."

"How did *that* happen?" I asked.

"I asked her that myself. 'Well, Roger,' she said, 'I used to be a sixth-grade teacher. Then I had a very strange experience.' Of course, I knew what the experience was, since I was part of it— but I couldn't tell her that, because I'm in disguise." He paused. "It's weird to talk to people I know without having them know it's me. Anyway, Ms. Schwartz said that after her experience she decided to make some changes in her life. The only thing she was certain of was that she wanted to continue to work with kids. After considering one thing and another, she ended up here."

"And my father?" I asked, feeling myself grow tense even as I managed to get the words out of my mouth.

Roger/Duncan shrugged. "He hasn't been the same since you left. But I don't know how he got hooked up with Ms. Schwartz. Maybe you should ask him yourself."

Fat chance, I thought. Then I realized that maybe I could.

After all, as long as I had my mask on, he would never even know it was *me* asking.

Duncan showed me the rooms along the hallway. They were all pretty much the same as the one where he was staying, with three bunk beds and three dressers. Sometimes they had posters on the walls and on the doors. They were all moderately neat. Then he took me to the kitchen, a huge room where they had pots big enough to sit in. A swinging door from the kitchen led back to the main room, where I had seen my father and Ms. Schwartz. We peeked around the door. The group was still meeting.

"Let me try to reach Broxholm again before we go out there," I whispered to Duncan.

He nodded, and we took a couple of steps backwards. I pulled out my URAT. To my relief, Broxholm answered almost at once. But no sooner had his face appeared on the screen than a voice behind me growled, "What's that? One of those pocket TVs? What're you looking at, a movie?"

Before I could answer, a dirty hand flashed over my shoulder and snatched the URAT away from me.

I spun around. "Give it back!" I bellowed, my heart pounding with several kinds of fear.

"Buzz off, you little weenie!" said the kid holding my URAT. He was a head taller than me, and had muscles on his muscles, which were easy to see since he was wearing a black T-shirt with the sleeves torn off. I noticed a lot of little burn marks on his forearms, and wondered what had driven him to run away from home.

"Ernie," said Duncan quietly, "why are you bothering my friend?"

"I ain't bothering him," said Ernie. "I just wanna look at his TV set."

"You're bothering him," said Duncan firmly.

"Well, I didn't mean to," said Ernie, starting to blush. "Here," he said, handing back the URAT. "Sorry."

"Thanks, Ernie," said Duncan.

"So, can I see it?" said Ernie politely. "I won't hurt it, I promise."

I was so astonished it took me a moment to answer. Finally I said, "Yeah, you can see it. But be careful. Here, let me set it up for you."

Broxholm and I had already worked out what to do if I got into a situation like this. I made a few adjustments to the URAT's controls, then handed it to Ernie. "It doesn't work very well," I said apologetically as I handed him a viewscreen showing a picture of "The Brady Bunch."

Suddenly the screen fuzzed and went blank—just as I had programmed it to do.

"Hey!" I yelled. "You broke it!"

"No, I didn't!" protested Ernie, handing it back to me. "I didn't do a thing, I swear!"

"Ernie, I'm really disappointed in you," said Duncan.

"I didn't do anything!" protested Ernie, louder than before.

Suddenly the door behind us swung open. "What's going on here?" asked a male voice.

I stuffed the URAT in my pocket. Turning, I found myself face to face with my father.

CHAPTER SIXTEEN

Catastrophe

I waited for him to recognize me, to say something, then remembered with a start that I was still wearing a mask.

"No real trouble, Mr. Thompson," said Duncan. "We had a disagreement, but it's been taken care of."

My father nodded. "Thank you, Roger. Care to introduce me to your friend?"

Duncan hesitated, then said, "This is Stoney."

"Does he need to stay here for a while?" asked my father.

"That's sort of up in the air," replied Duncan. "We'll know later this evening."

"Well, why don't the three of you come join us? The discussion is pretty interesting."

"I have to go to the bathroom first," I said. "I'll be there in a minute."

"Down that way and to the right," said my father.

I thanked him and practically ran in the direction he was pointing—not because I had to go to the bathroom, but because I wanted to get in touch

119

with Broxholm again. In the bathroom I whipped out my URAT and made the call. Broxholm's face appeared on the screen almost instantly.

"What happened? Are you all right?"

"Slight problem. Nothing major. I have—"

"Good. We're in the middle of something ourselves. But I've got a fix on your location now. We'll come get you as soon as possible."

He broke off the connection. I figured they must have something pretty intense going on. I was a little worried, but I thought they could probably handle whatever it was.

I wandered slowly back through the kitchen. I wasn't quite ready to sit in that group with my father and Ms. Schwartz. I wanted to figure out how I felt about the idea of their dating each other first. But I couldn't; it was too weird to make sense of.

Finally I went and joined the circle. A bunch of tough-looking boys and girls, most of them older than me, were talking about how they had been treated at home, or why their parents had thrown them out.

I sat and listened quietly. It was terrific to see Ms. Schwartz again; she was the best teacher I've ever had, and I had forgotten how much I loved her. (I know you're not supposed to say that kind of thing, but I *have* learned a lot from the aliens.)

I wondered how she would react if she knew Broxholm was on his way there that very minute.

Finally I looked at my father.

He was skinnier than when I had left, and his eyes were sad. But he looked a little healthier than the memory of him that I had stumbled across once when I was hooked into Duncan's mind.

What is he doing here! I wondered.

The discussion was interrupted by a pounding at the door. Several people jumped to their feet. Before anyone could make it to the door, it burst open and Broxholm staggered in. Susan lay stretched across his arms, her head hanging limply to the side. A trickle of blood ran along her cheek.

Broxholm's grief and rage were clear even through his mask. Kreeblim was limping behind him, her clothes torn and muddy.

"What happened?" I cried, leaping to my feet.

"We were attacked," said Kreeblim.

I ran to them, as did everyone else in the room. My father reached out and took Susan from Broxholm's arms. Broxholm swayed; for a moment I thought he was going to fall over. Then he spotted Ms. Schwartz. His eyes widened in surprise. She didn't know it was him, of course—he was wearing a different face than the last time she had seen him. Besides, her attention was all on Susan, though for that matter she didn't know it was Susan, either, since she was also wearing a mask.

"Bring her in here, Rod," Ms. Schwartz said to my father, walking toward a corridor I hadn't been down yet. My father followed her. So did Kreeblim and Broxholm. So did I. So did everyone else in the room.

"Please, kids, stay back!" said Ms. Schwartz. "You can't help by crowding."

Most of the kids started to drop back. But I walked on. So did Duncan.

"I asked you to stay back," said Ms. Schwartz.

"He comes," said Kreeblim, pointing at me.

Ms. Schwartz looked at me oddly, then shrugged. "Come along," she said. I could tell she didn't know what was going on but figured it wasn't worth a fight at the moment.

"Him, too," I said, pointing at Duncan.

Ms. Schwartz nodded and led the way to a small room. It looked like a school nurse's office, except it didn't have as much equipment. My father placed Susan gently on the cot. He knelt next to her, put a hand on her forehead, and listened to her breathe.

Ms. Schwartz began dialing the phone. Broxholm started to object, then fell silent.

"What happened?" asked my father.

"We were coming here to get . . . our friend," he said, gesturing to me. "We were tired, and therefore less watchful than we should have been. The riot downtown still has everyone stirred up; gangs of young people are roaming the streets. One of the gangs attacked us."

"They said, 'There's some aliens! Let's get them!' " whispered Kreeblim.

I wondered how a gang of kids could have known Broxholm and Kreeblim were aliens, until I realized that the gangs were probably just claiming that anyone who happened to look vulnerable was an alien in disguise, and using that as an excuse to attack.

I took some pleasure in imagining what would happen to any gang that attacked Broxholm. As I've said, he's the strongest being I've ever met. I had a feeling there were a lot of sorry teenagers out there.

"We managed to escape," continued Kreeblim, her voice bitter. "But one of the boys threw a rock that hit Susan here on the head."

"An ambulance is on the way," said Ms. Schwartz, putting down the phone. "It looks like you two could use some help as well."

"No!" said Broxholm.

My father and Ms. Schwartz blinked at the strength of his reaction. "No," he said again, his voice calmer. "No, we're all right." He turned toward my father. "How is the child?"

My father looked up. His face was grim, set.

"Not good," he whispered.

It wasn't until that moment that I realized Susan Simmons might die.

CHAPTER SEVENTEEN

Face-Off

When my father saw the look on my face he glanced at Ms. Schwartz. She nodded back, and he crossed to where I stood. "Come on, Stoney," he said, "let's talk a bit."

I nodded, though I didn't know how we would talk, since I didn't think I could speak at all. Susan Simmons was the best person I knew. Bright, funny, and kind, she had plenty of friends—yet she had been willing to be *my* friend when everyone else brushed me off as a geek. She was the only one who had ever tried to stop Duncan from beating me up (and had gotten herself a black eye in the process). She was a fighter for the good, the kind of kid who would change the world when she grew up, and I couldn't imagine the world without her.

My father led me into a little room with a desk, a couple of chairs, and a shabby couch. He sat me on the couch.

"I thought you were going to lose it there for a moment, pal," he said, trying to sound friendly.

He had never called me pal when I was his son.

I closed my eyes. "Susan is my best friend," I said.

He nodded. "I'm sure you wouldn't want to lose her." I heard an edge of pain in his voice, the sound of something catching in his throat.

"Did *you* ever lose someone you loved?" I asked.

He looked at me for a moment without answering, then nodded. "Several times."

Several times! What did that mean? My mother, maybe. And possibly me, though I found that hard to believe. But that didn't make "several." What was he talking about?

I realized that I knew hardly anything about him.

But then, he had never told me.

Of course, I had never asked. I had never had the chance before.

"Who did you lose, mister?"

He shook his head. "I don't like to talk about it."

I shrugged. "That's okay. I don't talk much about what I feel, either. It's safer that way."

He actually laughed then, though it was a small, sad sound. "Okay, Stoney, you nailed me. That's what I'm supposed to be working on these days—not holding so much inside. That's one of the reasons I'm here."

"What do you mean?" I asked. "Do you work here?"

"On a volunteer basis. That's my girlfriend in the other room. I started coming here to pick her up after work. Before I knew it, I was getting involved with some of the kids."

Why didn't you ever get involved with me! I wanted to scream. Instead I said calmly, "How did you meet her?"

I really wanted to know that, since he had never bothered to go to school events when I was living at home.

He looked at me for a moment, as if he was trying to decide how much to say. "How much do you know about this alien scare?" he asked at last.

"A little," I said cautiously.

"Ever hear of a kid named Peter Thompson?"

"Maybe. Was he on the news or something?"

"Not really. The authorities pretty much hushed things up. But rumors get around." He stood up and walked away from me. "Peter was about your age," he said, glancing out the window.

I tried to make my heart a stone. I knew I had to, or else I wouldn't be able to hear this, wouldn't be able to get through it without running from the room. And I *had* to hear, had to know what he would say.

"So, you knew this kid, Peter?" I prodded.

My father closed his eyes and whispered, "I was his father." Then he opened his eyes, looked

126

right into mine, and said, "Only I wasn't very good at it." He turned away again. "Why am I telling you this story?"

"To take my mind off my friend."

"Who are you?" he asked, reminding me of the number of times I had asked the same question of Hoo-Lan.

"Stoney."

He shrugged. "If that's all you want to tell for now, it's all right. That's one of the rules around here: we don't ask too much right away. Look, Stoney, I don't know if you've run away, how you're connected to those people in the other room, where your family is, anything about you. Even so, I'm going to tell you the rest of my story, because I think you ought to hear it. Maybe there's someone who loves you more than you think. Maybe there's a place you ought to go back to."

"Interesting idea," I replied.

"Peter Thompson was my son, and in my opinion he was just about the brightest kid who ever walked the face of the Earth. I loved him more than I can tell you. Only I never showed it very much. I didn't know how. Happens to some people, men especially. Happens when you never meet your father, and your mother dies when you're too old to get adopted. Happens when your wife takes off with another guy and you're left

127

with a kid you love but don't know how to raise."

He stopped and took a deep breath.

"I poured myself into my work. I figured that was good; I'd make money, and that would be a good way to love my kid, because he would have stuff that I never did. Except it wasn't good enough, because the one thing I had wanted most myself when I was a kid was exactly what I didn't give him. I didn't give him a father."

Stay stony, I told myself. *Keep your heart a stone or you'll never be able to endure this.*

"Anyway, this alien came to my kid's school. Peter and his friend—she was named Susan, like your friend in the other room there—they figured it out. But they couldn't get anyone to believe them."

His shoulders sagged. "Peter never even *tried* telling *me!* I wish he had. I get mad about that sometimes, mad that he didn't trust me, didn't give me a chance. Then I realize he had been giving me chances for years, but had finally given up.

"Well, Peter was a bright one, like I told you. He loved to read science fiction. That came from me. I gave him his first science fiction books."

I blinked. I had forgotten that!

"His one great dream was to explore other planets; he thought it was humankind's destiny.

128

So when his friend Susan figured out how to drive off the alien, what did Peter do?"

He paused, then announced in triumph, as if he knew I could never have guessed it, *"He went with him! My God,* do you realize how brave that kid was? What a thing to do!"

His eyes were shining with pride. He was proud—proud of *me!* I had never seen that before. I felt my stony heart begin to crack, begin to split inside me.

"For a long time I refused to believe what had really happened," he continued. "I thought Peter had just run away from home. I traveled all over the state looking for him, going to every kids' shelter I could find. That was how I met my girlfriend in there. See, she used to be Peter's teacher. But she left because of the alien thing, and so she was working at this place. When I came here looking for Peter, she finally convinced me of what had really happened. She knew him better than I did, I guess. She was pretty rough on me for a while, wouldn't let me forget what a jerk I had been with Peter. But even though she thought I was a clod, we had something in common. We had both lost something to the aliens."

He paused, then said, "Funny how the worst things in your life can lead to the best things."

"Sure is," I whispered.

"Anyway, I guess the real reason I'm here, the

reason I'm trying to help some of these kids, is that I hope if I do, maybe someone, somewhere, will help my boy, too. It's my bargain with the universe, Stoney. I don't know if the universe will hold up its end, if anyone ever *will* help Peter. But it's the best I can do."

He paused, then looked me in the eye again. "Let me tell you something, kid: if you love someone, don't keep it a secret. Don't ever let them get away from you without making sure they know that you care. I wish . . ." he choked a bit here, and the tears started to roll down his cheeks. "I wish I had told Peter."

The stone that used to be my heart cracked in two.

"You just did, Dad," I whispered.

Putting my fingers to my neck, I began to pull my mask from my face.

My father stared at me in astonishment. I could see his lips begin to tremble. Then I lost sight of him for a second, as I stripped the mask over my head. When I could see him again his whole face was twisted with a joy so deep it was almost pain.

"Peter!" he whispered.

He held out his hands.

I ran to him, and buried my head against his chest. Though I had sworn I wouldn't, I started to cry.

My father cried, too. He held me tight, and I

could feel him shaking as he wept for me, and for himself, and for everything that we had both lost, and then found again.

I didn't have the heart, then, to tell him that this might be Earth's last day.

CHAPTER EIGHTEEN

E Pootibus Unum

My father and I had a million things to say to each other, a million things to explain, to forgive. But before we could really start, before we could do more than hold each other for a minute, the ambulance arrived.

At the sound of the sirens, we raced out of the room where we had been talking, back toward the nurse's office. We didn't make it inside; the paramedics were there, and it was too crowded for anyone else to enter.

Dad put his arm around my shoulders. We didn't wait long; less than five minutes had gone by when I heard a wail from Ms. Schwartz. Three paramedics came out of the room. Two of them, a man and a woman, were carrying a stretcher between them. On it lay Susan's pale, unmoving body.

My father reached out and touched the third paramedic on the arm. "Is she . . ."

The man shook his head. "Not yet," he said softly. "But we don't have much hope."

Susan!

I buried my face against my father's chest and began to sob again.

But something weird was happening. I wasn't sure how I was aware of it. I didn't see anything, didn't hear anything. But I knew it anyway, in some place deep inside of me.

"What is *that?*" cried the man my father had spoken to.

Spinning around, I saw a jellylike blob oozing its way down the hallway. It stopped for a moment and lifted a pair of eyestalks. "Poot!" it cried.

Another poot was coming right behind it, and another after that. Turning, I saw them coming from the other direction, too. Kids were running into the hallway, crying, "Come back! Poot, come back!"

"Peter, what's going on?" asked my father.

Before I could answer, the head of the ambulance team yelled, "Come on, let's get out of here!"

"I'm sorry," said Broxholm. "I can't let you do that."

He was standing in the door of the medical office, holding a little tube that looked like pencil. Unlike a pencil, it could melt a door shut. Of course, the people from the ambulance didn't know that yet. They paused, but you could tell they were on the verge of bolting.

"What's stopping us?" asked the leader of the team.

"Let me put it as a request," said Broxholm evenly. "We need some time. Please bring the child back into the office."

Poots were coming from all directions now, sometimes on their own, sometimes being carried by puzzled-looking kids. All of them were heading toward the little medical office.

"We need time," repeated Broxholm.

"Let's go," said the woman holding the front of the stretcher. She began walking toward the door.

"Wait!"

Reaching up with one hand, Broxholm began to peel off his mask, revealing the lime-green skin and huge orange eyes underneath. Kids screamed. One of the men turned white and looked as if he was about to faint. My father drew me closer—though whether he was afraid of Broxholm or afraid I might go off with him again, I wasn't certain.

The shock tactic worked. "What do you want?" asked the ambulance woman nervously as a steady line of poots oozed past her.

"Just some time," said Broxholm. "Something is happening, I don't know what. But we need to let it happen. I promise we will not hurt you while you are here if you will just take Susan back into the office."

I thought that was clever of him. They might blow up the planet later, but they weren't going to hurt the people while they were still here in the shelter.

And still the poots kept coming. Duncan and his friends had been busy. There were hundreds of them.

"Peter," whispered my father, "what are these things?"

"Poots!"

"What are they doing?"

"I don't have the faintest idea."

The paramedics were still hesitating. Broxholm moved a finger, and a burst of light from the pencil-like thing burned a hole in the wall just above one paramedic's head.

"Please bring Susan back into the office," he repeated.

Without a word, the paramedics did as he asked. Poots oozed their way in alongside them. After a moment Kreeblim called, "Peter, I think you should come in here."

My father let go of me, and I pushed my way into the medical office, stepping over half a dozen poots to do so. Duncan was kneeling beside Susan's body, crying. Ms. Schwartz was standing nearby, her face shifting between sorrow and fear.

"Peter, I'm going out there to help Broxholm keep things in line," said Kreeblim. "You stay here with Susan."

"Broxholm?" cried Ms. Schwartz, her voice sharp with fear. Then she saw me, saw my true face without its mask, and the look on her own face changed again. *"Peter?* Oh, Peter, your father will be so happy!"

"I suppose there's not much need for this anymore," said Duncan. Working gently, he peeled off the mask that covered Susan's face. Then, with Ms. Schwartz still speechless in astonishment, he removed his own mask as well.

I went to kneel beside Susan.

I could hear Broxholm and Kreeblim in the hall, trying to decide how to keep people from leaving the building until we could get a decent head start.

I stopped worrying about them when I saw what the poots were doing.

It started when two poots met in the center of the room and flowed together. Soon a third joined them, and then a fourth. The poots flowing into the room moved straight toward the blob in the center of the floor. It continued to grow as poot after poot joined the gelatinous mass, making it two, three, four feet long.

And still the poots kept coming, by ones and twos and dozens, until finally we found ourselves facing an eight-foot poot.

Ms. Schwartz was standing behind me, her hands on my shoulders. "Peter," she whispered, "what's going on?"

"I don't know. Just watch."

The mass on the floor seemed to writhe for a while, smoothing out lumps in its surface. I could see material flowing inside it, as if it was rearranging itself. Suddenly it thrust out a pair of stalks, each about as thick as my forearm, and bellowed, "POOT!"

Then it began to glide toward Susan's body.

"Duncan, get back!" I yelled.

Duncan looked at me dully for a moment, then jumped away from the cot. The giant poot moved to the end of the cot and reared back, so that it was taller than I am. Then it fell onto Susan. As we watched in fascinated horror it engulfed her body, like an amoeba absorbing a bit of food. For a terrifying moment I thought it *was* eating her. I could see her shape through the creature's sides, as if I were viewing her through a piece of glass smeared with Vaseline.

Before I could catch my breath a voice behind me said, "We have to go now."

"Sharleen!" said Ms. Schwartz. "What are *you* doing here? And what do you mean, you have to go?"

"Ms. Schwartz, I really like you," said Sharleen. "So try not to let this upset you too much, all right?"

Then Hoo-Lan reached up and pulled off his mask. I could tell how much of a shock his blue-

skinned, big-eyed face was to Ms. Schwartz from the way her fingers dug into my shoulder.

"It's all right," I said, trying to sound reassuring. "He's my teacher."

"How wonderful," Ms. Schwartz replied in a weak voice.

"We have to go," repeated Hoo-Lan. "Kreeblim has called the saucer. It's overhead now, and will be touching down in the vacant lot next door as soon as we're all outside."

"What about my father?" I asked, a feeling of panic clutching my heart.

Hoo-Lan hesitated, then sighed. "It is unlikely I can get myself into any more trouble than I already have. I invite him to come. You too, Ms. Schwartz."

Ms. Schwartz looked at Duncan and me. I smiled at her. "No force fields," I said. "Right, Hoo-Lan?"

"A promise," he said, holding up his hand. "You will be safe as long as Earth itself is."

At the moment, that wasn't much of a promise. But it seemed to be good enough for Ms. Schwartz. "I'll come," she whispered.

I could tell she was terrified. I understood that the real reason she was coming was to watch out for us three kids.

Kreeblim shouldered her way past Hoo-Lan and touched the end of the giant poot with a metal stick. The megapoot seemed to have gone totally inert. When Kreeblim lifted the stick, the huge creature (Susan included) floated into the air.

"That's it," said Kreeblim fiercely. "We're going."

Feeling gloomier than I could ever remember, I walked between my father and Ms. Schwartz to the saucer.

We docked the saucer in the chamber beneath the barn. Using her antigravity wand, Kreeblim carried Susan's poot-wrapped body through the tunnel Broxholm and I had dug and into the farmhouse. In the kitchen she set the poot-pod down on the long farm table.

We all gathered around to stare at it.

"WHAT IS HAPPENING?" rumbled Big Julie.

"I'll go explain," said Hoo-Lan. "He might as well learn that I'm back in the game."

Broxholm looked grateful.

"What *is* happening?" asked my father nervously.

"I do not know," Kreeblim replied, her nose slapping back and forth in deep distress. "This kind of poot behavior has never been recorded before."

It was the longest evening of my life.

"You do realize," said Broxholm, late in the day, after we had explained all our adventures to my father and Ms. Schwartz, "that tomorrow we must return to the *New Jersey* to file our final report?"

"We haven't found much hope, have we?" I whispered.

"More than I expected," said Broxholm.

"Yet not enough, I fear," said Kreeblim. "Rightly or not, today's events will confirm the council's worst fears. Your distrust of outsiders is so great, so deep, that I don't see how you can ever enter the community of planets."

"Will it be—The Button?" asked Duncan.

Kreeblim closed her middle eye. Her hair flat in a sign of mourning, she said, "I fear the worst."

CHAPTER NINETEEN

Meeting of the Minds

There was no sleep for me that night. Even if I hadn't been terrified about what was happening to my best friend, I would have been kept awake by the gut-turning fact that human life was about to end because we had failed in our mission.

One of those lives was that of my father, who was resting, probably as sleepless as I, in the room next door.

I couldn't bear the thought of losing him now that we had finally connected.

And so many mysteries remained unsolved. What was the meaning of the vision I had experienced in the council chamber just before they sent us back to Earth? For that matter, what was the meaning of the vision I had experienced when I connected with Hoo-Lan's brain back in the *New Jersey* when CrocDoc was examining my brain? Why had Hoo-Lan been dressed as a teacher? Why had I "seen" him destroy a television set in an act of sheer rage? And why had he been so frightened when I asked him about it that he had practically begged me not to tell anyone else?

I was considering going to his room and insisting that he explain it all when I heard Susan whisper, *Peter? Peter, is that you?*

"Susan?"

I sat up in bed.

But the room was empty.

Peter? she repeated. This time I realized that her voice was inside my head.

I'm here! I thought joyfully, feeling the same kind of connection I had felt with Duncan when Hoo-Lan's machines helped me form a telepathic link to him, back when he was imprisoned in Kreeblim's force field.

In fact, Duncan was the next to speak—or think, as the case may be.

Hey, I'm here, too! he said.

What's going on? asked Susan.

You've got me! I replied. *We thought you were dead. Then hundreds of poots got together and scarfed you up. Now here you are, inside my head.*

Our heads, corrected Duncan.

I could feel Susan's relief as she thought, *So I'm not dead, right?*

I sure hope not! I replied.

But you are wrapped inside the biggest poot in the history of the universe, added Duncan.

I felt a surge of panic, then realized it wasn't

my panic, but Susan's, which I was experiencing as completely as if it were my own. *I can't move!* she thought.

As I tried to send her feelings of calmness I felt another mind trying to join us. It was struggling to get in, as if there were some wall it could not pass. It was Hoo-Lan! I could feel his frustration and his sorrow that he was not able to connect to the melding of minds that had happened between us. His thoughts came through in bits and pieces—things about *congratulations*, and *well done*, and *moment of triumph*.

I went after him, to try to bring him into our meeting of minds. But I couldn't find him.

Duncan, help me, I thought. *We need to get him into this. There are things I want to know from him.*

I can help, too, thought Susan.

I understood, without her having to tell me, that by working with us she would feel less afraid.

When I knew that, I suddenly understood that if I wanted, I could see/experience/understand *everything* about Susan or Duncan.

And they could understand everything about me.

There were no secrets left. Our love and our hate were all in the open now. Every thought I had, whether good or evil, base or noble, was going to be available to them. I began to pull back, fearful at the thought of being known so fully.

Duncan held me with his mind. *Don't go!* he pleaded. *We need to stay connected for this.*

I surrendered. Together, it took us only a moment to reach out and pull Hoo-Lan into our union.

You did it! he thought in astonishment.

His thoughts were not as clear and open as the ones that passed between us three humans. Even so, he was right. We had managed to bring him in. Now, like us, he had no secrets. Yet he was still hard to understand, mostly because the information I was picking up didn't seem to make sense.

Finally I asked him flat out, *How old are you?*

His amusement rippled through my entire being. *That's a very hard question. The response depends on how you define age, time, and a lot of other things.*

I knew you wouldn't get a straight answer out of him, thought Duncan in disgust.

I'll give it to you as straight as I can manage, said Hoo-Lan seriously. *What complicates it is the way time gets wonky when you travel at great speed. Peter was on board the* New Jersey *for nearly five of your months, but he experienced it as a matter of mere weeks, because of the way time works at near light speed—not to mention what happens when you start making space-shifts. A lifetime of that sort of thing makes issues of age seriously strange.*

So how old are you? asked Susan, repeating my question.

I was born in the year 1013, as you reckon time.

But that would make you nearly a thousand years old! thought Duncan. His astonishment tickled through my brain.

It would, replied Hoo-Lan, *if not for the effects of space travel. In actuality, I have only experienced one hundred seventeen years—which makes me middle-aged by the standards of my people, by the way.*

And you've been interested in Earth for a long time, haven't you? I asked.

Hoo-Lan couldn't have lied if he had wanted to. I could feel his answer in every fiber of my being.

He decided to explain. *You know that I have long been on a quest for the direct mind-to-mind communication we are now experiencing.*

Though I could feel his twinges of jealousy that we were experiencing the connection more clearly and fully than he was, I could also sense his generous joy on our behalf.

Long before your planet came to the attention of the galaxy at large, I had concluded that this was the place it was most likely to happen.

So you were visiting us before the others knew about us?

I would tell you who thought that question, but I really don't know. We were so closely linked it could have been Susan, Duncan, me— or all of us at once.

I started way back, replied Hoo-Lan. The thought was ripe with amusement. *I started bending the noninvolvement rules then as well— not that I was always successful. I tried to convince Isabella not to give Columbus the money for those ships, for example. Too bad she wouldn't listen to me. I believe if the Native Americans had had a while longer on their own, they would have been far better prepared to deal with the European invasion. Well, I was only one being; I couldn't handle everything.*

I remembered some other things he had said to me, and I knew I was on the track of something— maybe even a lever we could use against the Interplanetary Council!

You finally broke the rules big time, didn't you? I asked. *You didn't just meddle. You did something worse.*

The combined sense of shame and rebellion that washed through us told me I had struck home.

Your science was hurtling forward far faster than your ability to deal with it. Without intervention, you would have made it into space long before you were ready. I was sure that the council would feel driven to just such measures as it is considering now. Only then the odds of them deciding to destroy you would have been even greater.

Susan and Duncan, linked to me, were following me into the nooks and crannies of Hoo-Lan's brain, digging for his secret. When we found it, we thought together, in astonishment, *So you showed us how to invent television!*

Hoo-Lan's shamed agreement echoed through our minds.

Finally I understood the vision I had experienced when CrocDoc had taken out my brain. Hoo-Lan had snuck into the lab during that time and tried to connect with my mind. He had been partially successful, and the images that I had experienced—the picture of him dressed as a teacher, destroying a television set in a fit of rage—were an expression of his own guilt over what he had done.

It was my great crime, confessed Hoo-Lan. *Even though I knew your species was nowhere near ready to deal with the power of such a communication tool, I carefully and slowly planted the seeds for it. I knew it would be bad for you, but I also knew that once the best brains of your world started turning themselves into Swiss cheese by watching the mind-rotting mush your people would produce, it would slow your sci-*

ence enough to give us a few more years to decide how to deal with you. I hoped that by
slowing you down for a bit I could give your
basic being-ness a chance to catch up with your
technology. I hoped you could be welcomed into
the galaxy as a civilized people.

I remembered Broxholm telling me that Earth's
science had been mysteriously sidetracked a few
decades ago. At last I knew what had done it!

What I didn't anticipate, continued Hoo-Lan,
was the degree to which you would abuse television. I began to feel as if I had given a loaded
gun to an innocent child, thinking that it was
only a water pistol. I do not know how to make
up for it.

I do, I replied.

And then I told them my plan to save the
world.

CHAPTER TWENTY

"One Is All, and All Are One"

Toward morning a wild cry rang through the farmhouse. I knew what had happened. Even so, I ran to the kitchen, as did everyone else.

Kreeblim, who had been keeping watch, was staring in astonishment at the table where Susan lay, twitching and moaning, but very much alive.

On the floor next to the table lay a dry, clear husk that looked like a lot of crumpled cellophane—all that was left of the giant poot that had absorbed and healed her, and led us into telepathic union.

Kreeblim's own poot, which had been resting in a Tupperware container in the refrigerator at the moment of the great poot merger, was lying at the edge of the pootskin. "Poot," it muttered in such a mournful tone that it nearly broke my heart. "Poot poot poot poot poot!"

But how could my heart break when one of the two people I knew best in all the world, a person as close to me as myself, was alive and well?

A moment later Susan opened her eyes and smiled.

"I'm here!" she said.

And here, I thought, putting my hand to my heart, to my head.

She nodded, because she could understand me, hear me, without a word being said.

So the early morning was a party, and we celebrated Susan as the sun rose and filled the room with light.

But the late morning was different, because it was time for us to return to the stars and file our final report.

Hoo-Lan came to me shortly before noon, smiling so broadly I was afraid he might hurt his face. "I contacted CrocDoc this morning and told him what happened last night. He put it together with everything that he had already figured out from his studies of your brain, and ran the whole mass of data through the computer again."

"And?" I asked, eagerly.

Hoo-Lan's smile got even wider. "Your brain may have saved the world."

Two hours later we stood before the Interplanetary Council, ready to plead for the life of our planet. My father was with us, as was Ms. Schwartz.

My heart was pounding. I had never particularly liked speaking in public. Now I had to speak to the galaxy—and do it well enough to convince them not to use The Button.

Fortunately, the others went first, starting with Hoo-Lan. "As you know," he said, "I have long had a special interest in the planet in question."

"An unhealthy interest, oh former Prime Member," said Shadow from the corner.

"That is a personal judgment," Hoo-Lan replied sharply. "In point of fact, my interest has turned out to be well justified."

"Why?" screeched Bat-thing.

Hoo-Lan smiled. "Because in the people of Earth I have discovered a species unique in the galaxy. By our own rules, this species must be protected until more study is done on it."

"They are unique in their destructiveness," bubbled Red Seaweed. "What else makes them unusual?"

"Just this," said Hoo-Lan. *"There is only one of them."*

The flurry of concern and puzzlement that rippled through the council was expressed in as many different ways as there were beings. Shadow almost disappeared. Red Seaweed's stalks began to shoot up and down. The being with purple tentacles shivered so violently that the drops of mist being sprayed over it spattered in all directions. (Of course, since it was only a holographic projection, the drops didn't actually land on any of the other council members.)

"What exactly do you mean?" asked the sea-green alien who towered above the others.

"Nikka, nikka, flexxim puspa," said Hoo-Lan, speaking for himself the words, the guess, that he had sent through my lips in this very chamber three weeks earlier. Only this time I understood the phrase more precisely. It was not "One for all and all for one." It was, "One *is* all and all *are* one."

"That describes the human condition precisely," continued Hoo-Lan. "For though it is housed in many separate bodies, there is only one human being. It is a single, vast, interconnected organism."

"Do you have any proof of this?" asked Red Seaweed.

CrocDoc stepped forward. "My studies of Peter Thompson's brain indicated that this might be the case. However, I lacked confirmation for such a strange theory until this morning, when Hoo-Lan informed me of a new situation that had developed."

"The situation had to do with me," said Susan. "I was injured, and in danger of dying, when I was encased by a giant poot."

"It may well be that the poots represent the same phenomenon of a many and a one," said Kreeblim. "But their intellect is at such a low level that we never became aware of it."

"But being inside this giant poot somehow opened my mind, so that I could be connected with Peter and Duncan," continued Susan.

153

"Our minds had already been opened some because of things that Hoo-Lan had tried with us," Duncan added.

That stirred up the council again. Hoo-Lan waited for them to calm down, then said, "They were able to allow me inside the connection as well. Based on that experience of their minds, I am convinced that the single-organism theory is correct. It explains a lot—as Duncan will tell you."

Duncan blushed. "Well, I have a lot of science and history in my head, because of Kreeblim frying my brain last month," he said. "Putting it all together, it looks to me as if early in our evolution we developed barriers to keep our individual mind units separate, because it was too hard to cope with having them all connected. I believe that as humans developed, the totally open link became too painful. Complete awareness of every unit of the being, the numbers of which were growing rapidly, was so overwhelming that those able to block it had an advantage in going on with their individual lives.

"Blocking the connection became a survival trait. With the passing of time, over millions of years, nearly everyone blocked the connection. We survived, but the cost was a never-ending sense of loss and separation. The one had become many."

I remembered what Big Julie had said the first

day we met him: "WHAT WAS ONE CAN BE-COME MANY. WHAT WAS MANY CAN BE-COME ONE. YOU JUST HAVE TO KNOW HOW TO DO IT."

Broxholm pulled his nose. "This pain, this loss, is at the core of all their craziness," he said sadly. "They are angry, but they don't know why. They mourn, but they don't know the cause. They ache for a loss they do not understand, and their solace is but momentary. And when they lash out, they cannot feel the pain they cause."

"Of course, this is only a theory," said Hoo-Lan gleefully. "We will have to spend *years* studying it to make sure that this is really the case."

Years in which they can't destroy us, I thought happily.

Amen! thought Susan, taking my hand.

Hoo-Lan spoke again. "The human mind, when open, was more open than any mind in the galaxy. Painfully open. In an attempt to change, it became stuck closed. If we can help them learn to work both ways, to open and close as necessary, we will have a great ally. Toward this end, I want to let my friend and student, Peter Thompson, make a suggestion."

It was my turn at last. My father squeezed my arm. Then I stood and faced the galaxy.

I knew my words and my image were being broadcast to planets beyond my imagination. Beings across the galaxy were watching me, judging me—and through me, Earth.

Our survival seemed likely—for now, at least.

But I didn't want mere survival. I wanted us to be given the chance to take our rightful place among the stars.

You can do it! thought Susan.

We're with you, Duncan told me.

I began to speak.

CHAPTER TWENTY-ONE

The Master Plan

"Beings of the galaxy," I said, "I come to you as a representative of a troubled people, to speak of a crime committed against us. My friend and teacher Hoo-Lan committed this crime, a crime forbidden by your own laws. He has agreed to let me speak to you of it and seek compensation."

I paused while the eight members of the council made their various expressions of dismay.

"Here is what happened," I continued when they were quiet again. "Years ago Hoo-Lan secretly slipped us information on how to create television, a technology for which we were not ready. This intrusion by the being who was once Prime Member of your council has caused great damage among my people. Therefore, I now wish to file a claim on behalf of the people of Earth, seeking total restitution for the mental capacity lost to television."

The council members all began to talk at once. I waited until Red Seaweed had called them back to order.

"What is your request?" it asked, sounding as though it had a fish caught in its throat.

"Give us teachers," I said to him, to the galaxy. His stalks shot out in astonishment. *"What?"*

"I ask you to send us teachers. Though we have discovered the truth about our minds, merely knowing that we are all connected is not going to solve our problems. We need to learn to reopen that connection. We need to harness our power. We need help doing that. Send us teachers, the best you have, because teachers and children can change the world. Send thousands of them—hundreds of thousands, if you can find them. If you do, then perhaps in twenty or thirty or forty years, we of Earth may finally be ready to take our rightful place in the universe."

The aliens sent us out of the chamber while they discussed my suggestion.

"Oh, Peter," said my father, putting his arm around me. "That was well done. I am so proud of you."

After two of the most frightening hours I have ever spent, the aliens called us back to the council chamber.

"Krepta," said the purple-tentacled alien, "we have discussed your suggestion. We want to know this: will you be willing to stay on Earth to help with this mission?"

I stared at him. Stay on Earth? When all I had ever wanted was to go to the stars?

159

But I had seen the stars. I had been to another planet.

And I had found something else, the thing I had wanted most of all, from before the time I had met Broxholm.

I had my father back.

More than that, I had been made a witness to the best and worst of what we are. I knew things that had to be shared. I knew, from my visit to Hoo-Lan's planet, that peace was possible. I knew, too, the terrible things on Earth that needed to be changed.

I looked at the aliens.

"Earth is my home," I whispered. "I will stay and help."

"Then we will send the teachers," said Red Seaweed. "And eagerly await the day when Earth is ready to join us."

The first group of teachers arrives this summer. They have to stay in disguise, of course, until Earth is better able to deal with the idea. But it's the beginning. So if you get a teacher who's a little unusual next year, a teacher who expects a lot from you—well, who knows?

Maybe you just got a tough cookie.

Or maybe you've got someone who is preparing you for a trip to the stars.

But you don't need to worry.

This time around, it won't be by kidnapping.

It will be by invitation.

The Last Words

I thought it might be embarrassing to be totally connected, to know everything, to have everything known. But that's only when you're being silly. It's only when you're afraid of your body and what you are. It's only when you try to hide from nature and won't accept yourself.

The truth is, it's not embarrassing, it's beautiful. And I didn't know how lonely I was until I wasn't alone anymore.

I'm not alone now even though Susan and Duncan are traveling the stars with the aliens. We're still connected.

I could have gone, too, of course. I have a place among them.

But I've already been there, and I'm needed here, to help the aliens. Besides, I have a home now, with my father and his new wife, my new mother, Ms. Schwartz.

My name is Peter Thompson.
But it is also Duncan Dougal.
And Susan Simmons.

About the Author
and Illustrator

Bruce Coville has written dozens of books for young readers, including *My Teacher Is an Alien*, *My Teacher Fried My Brains*, *Monster of the Year*, and the Camp Haunted Hills books, *How I Survived My Summer Vacation*, *Some of My Best Friends Are Monsters*, and *The Dinosaur That Followed Me Home*. He grew up in central New York, where he's lived most of his life. Before becoming a full-time writer, Bruce Coville worked as a magazine editor, a teacher, a toymaker, and a gravedigger. He currently lives in Manhattan.

John Pierard is best known for his illustrations for *Isaac Asimov's Science Fiction Magazine*, *Distant Stars*, and several books in the *Time Machine* series. He has most recently illustrated *My Babysitter Is a Vampire* and *My Teacher Fried My Brains*. He lives in Manhattan.